Faith under Shellfire

Journal of the last months of
World War II in Waxweiler, Germany

By Viktor Kiefer, Priest in Waxweiler from 1936-1945

Translated by Uta (Irsch) Milewski

Faith under Shellfire
Journal of the last months of World War II in Waxweiler
By Viktor Kiefer
Translated by Uta (Irsch) Milewski

First Edition, German 1989 © Volksbildungswerk Waxweiler
Seelsorge im Kugelhagel
Erlebnisbericht über die letzten Monate des Krieges
von Pfarrer V. Kiefer

Second Edition, English 2020 © Uta Milewski
Faith under Shellfire
Published by Love Joy Publishing
Published in English by permission of Klaus Juchmes,
Voksbildungswerk Waxeiler 1989

Print ISBN Number   978-0-9820062-3-8
Ebook ISBN Number   978-0-9820062-4-5

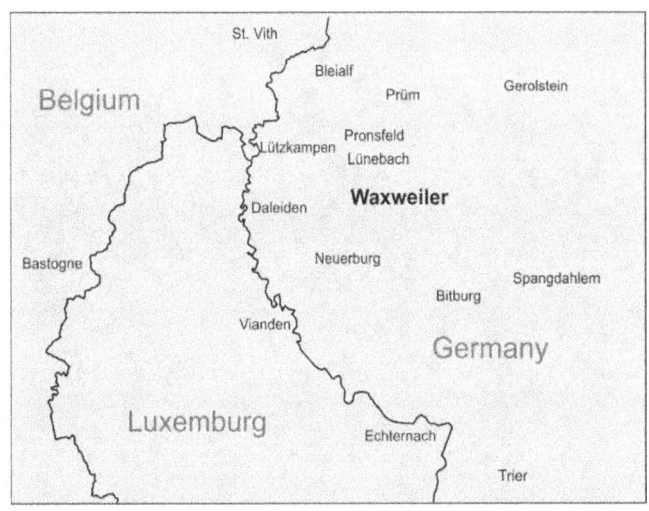

Belgium/Luxemburg/Germany Border Region

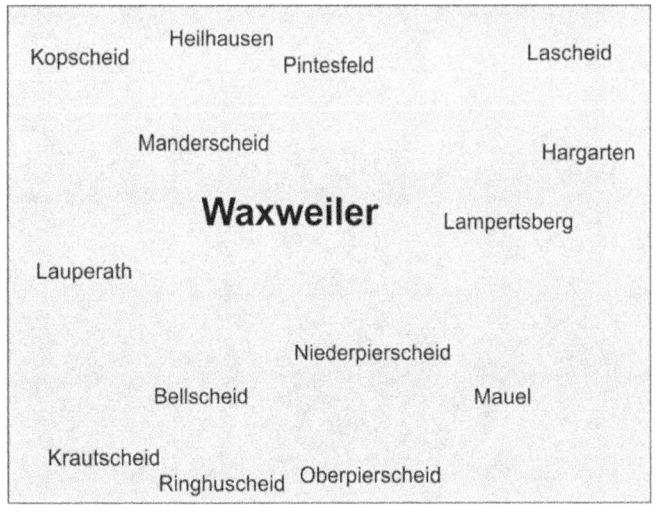

Waxweiler and surrounding Villages

Biography of Reverend Kiefer

Aug 18, 1898	born in Heiligenwald, Germany
1904 – 1908	Heiligenwald Elementary School
1908 – 1916	St. Wendel High School
1919 – 1923	Study of Theology in Trier
1923 – 1927	Chaplain in Engers
1927 – 1929	Chaplain in Heimersheim/Ahr
1929 – 1933	Chaplain in Betzdorf/Sieg
1933 – 1936	Priest in Preischeid
1936 – 1945	Priest in Waxweiler
1945 – 1950	Priest in Niedermendig
1950 – 1960	Priest in Püttlingen
1960 – 1969	Priest in Heddesheim (now Guldental)
August 1969	Retired in Kreuznach
1981	Deceased in Kreuznach, final resting place in home parish of Heilingwald

Journal of the last months of the war

by Viktor Kiefer
Pastor in Waxweiler from 1936-1945

September 3, 1944

After an incredibly rapid advance of the American tanks through France, our German troops soon reach the Luxemburg/German border in constant retreat before the imposing enemy. This morning at about nine o'clock the first cars drive through our town of Waxweiler at breakneck speed. Soon there is gridlock, and I ask one of the drivers: "Are you *going to* the front or are you *coming from* the front?" Depressed, he answered: "We come from the front." So, these are the first columns of the receding army of the Third Reich! A feeling of joy overtakes me about the approaching end of the war and thus of the Third Reich, the approaching freedom after twelve years of stress and oppression. Soon more vehicles arrive. Cars and trucks follow each other in an unbroken chain. Some are rear coupled and pulled along for lack of fuel. The troops are still in pretty good shape. This is the first unit that makes its way out of the mess. Today is our annual town fair, and the passing troops are served coffee and cake. Just like during pre-war fairs, there's a hustle and bustle on the Kanal, the central square in town. Almost all the boys of the town are there. While the military drivers get directions for their retreat, the boys climb in droves all over the vehicles. They ride along, singing and screaming into the next town up the hill and then come running back, laughing and screaming to ride along again a second and third time. For them it's just like the usual fair rides of carousel and swings. The mood is joyful and expectant. Everybody feels that important decisions will be made in the next few days. Eight days ago, the Third

Reich called every man to service. To the last contingent every man and boy from the ages of 15 to 65 has to be ready to go to the dreaded war front. "Now for good" is the propaganda issued by the Nazis, which finds little echo in the people. The bulwark of the dictatorship is crumbling away.

September 4, 1944

Yesterday towards the evening, a small unit stopped in town. Armored trucks now stand under the chestnut trees on the Trierer Strasse, which provide camouflage from the fighters overhead. The troops have been quartered in individual homes nearby. They are all young guys; they wear the uniform and badges of the Waffen-SS.

September 10, 1944

The young troops are still here. In the course of the week the news leaked: It is the small remnant of Panzer Division "Hitler Youth" which has been almost completely wiped out. Not a single tank is left, only half a dozen other vehicles. Allegedly the squad is waiting for fuel to continue the retreat. During the week, I had the opportunity to talk to two boys of the division. One was from the nearby Daun area, so he was an "Eifler." Forced to join the SS; otherwise they seem okay. Both are happy that they'll return to their mothers soon.

September 11, 1944

At noon, the first troops come from the opposite direction. They are several hundred men in infantry units. They come on foot from Trier, running in double time. Their mission is to occupy the bunkers of the Westwall (Siegfried Wall). It's an exceptionally hot September day. During a rest stop, the soldiers collapse on the side of the road and appeal for drinking water. Their mood is depressed. When I pass by, I am often asked, "How far is it to the border?" I come into conversation with a noncommissioned officer, who is from the Saar valley. He thinks all is lost. His only wish is for the Americans to come soon and "cash in" which means to capture them as POW's. The troops use the direct route to the front, regardless of difficulties and being visible to fighter planes.

So far no enemy plane has been seen except for the overflights of the big bomber units to which we are already accustomed. When I point out a safer and easier way to travel, that offers good tree-cover from fighters, all I get is a rant and a rave on the stubbornness of the higher-ups.

We have a pastors' meeting in the nearby village of Ringhuscheid this afternoon. On the way we hear artillery in close proximity for the first time. In Ringhuscheid we talk about the events of the last few days. Everyone is happy. We soon expect the end of the war and with that, the end of the Third Reich. In the middle of the conversation, a divisional military chaplain bursts out: "Well, gentlemen, you're sitting here so comfortably together and meanwhile the American tanks are rolling into your parishes!"

The chaplain told us that his troop, a Panzer Division, was the last one in touch with the Americans when they crossed the border and were now heading for the Rhine without any tanks. The division had orders to gather again on the other side of the Rhine. The chaplain's words were confirmed by the renewed dull roars of shells striking nearer than before. In fact, the Americans occupied the first frontier villages on the Luxembourg-Belgian border that afternoon without any resistance. The Westwall was virtually unoccupied. After the events of the last weeks, we were expecting the Americans to move into our towns and villages, at least by the next day. When I came home late in the afternoon, I found Waxweiler in turmoil: The Kreisleiter, the head Nazi of the county, had pulled up in his fancy limousine and had his family packed up and taken away. The Kreisleiter and the families who were moving to safety were hackled by a mob that had formed right in front of their house, something unheard of in the Third Reich.

Shortly thereafter the first refugees arrived from the border with terrible news: Since noon the border villages are under American artillery fire. Many houses are burning. It was like a cold rain on our happy parade. Maybe the end won't go so smoothly and the war with all its horrors will still haunt us? More desperate than before, we were even more anxiously awaiting the Americans to move through quickly. Full of uncertainty and tension, we all anticipate the coming night.

September 12, 1944

The mother and sister of the pastor of Daleiden, one of the border towns, arrives to lodge with me. "For a few days," my colleague says as he brings his relatives in. We are all convinced that everything will be over in a few days, and then everything goes back to normal, with the big difference, of course, that we will once again be free citizens and the nightmare of National Socialism will finally disappear. Yet we pity the people farther inland from the border, who still have to endure all that we have already overcome.

September 13, 1944

The night has actually passed without major incident! Around noon, the Ortsgruppenleiter, the head Nazi of the town, is visibly pleased that an American scout car had been shot at in the night about an hour from here. The American scout retreated behind the bunker line. During the day, an artillery lieutenant and his underling park in my rectory courtyard.

They are waiting for supplies and troops to make a defensive maneuver beyond the Kyll river about 20 miles to the East. Gradually the fear begins to grow in us, that Germany could gather a resistance on the Western front. To be sure, we have not yet given up hope of a speedy resumption of the Americans' advance. As a soldier of the First World War, I know only too well what a hardening of the front in the Westwall area would mean for us.

September 15, 1944

After two days without significant events, today was both exciting and distressing. Yesterday evening trucks brought several hundred combat engineers, men and boys from Mayen County. They had been deployed at the Saar river, but were pulled back because of excessive artillery fire. Now they were here to set up a defensive resistance line in the hills around the Prüm river that crosses through our steep valley. In the excitement of the previous few weeks it had escaped our notice that train traffic on our small rail spur had stopped. We were too busy to think about trains, but this morning, an empty train had arrived to evacuate railroad workers and their families. The families would be taken to the Thuringia region, whereas the railway workers themselves were needed in the town of Gerolstein, the hub or our rail spur.

Towards the end of the morning's school chapel service, a mother rushes into the church excitedly to quickly pull her children from the pews. At first I didn't think anything of it except that maybe the Americans were moving in. Later I discover that it was one of the railroad worker families and they were supposed to be on the train that was about to leave.

The combat engineers who had arrived the evening before stand restlessly in the street outside of the church. Nobody pays them any attention. I advise the townspeople to go home immediately, which many do.

All sorts of unsubstantiated rumors run through the town. Everywhere there are groups, mostly women huddled together. Almost the entire male population had left for 14 days to build up defenses. We discover later, they had been taken to the Saargan, on the Lorraine-Luxembourg border.

In the afternoon at about three o'clock suddenly the announcement comes: Everyone is to come to the Adolf Hitler Square across from the rectory. The mayor announces that a train had delivered ammunition and will depart empty. Whoever wants, can leave. In the shortest possible time, those concerned would have to be at the station. Indescribable restlessness and indecision now seize many, but few are able to pack their suitcases in time to meet the train. They all return shortly, a little embarrassed. The train had not waited, but left shortly after unloading the ammunition. Visibly pleased to be relieved of the decision, the more ambivalent people breath a breath of relief. Without any hesitation I am determined to stay in town at any cost, whatever the outcome.

Suddenly renewed unrest: in countless columns several thousand foreigners arrive. They are mostly Polish men in ragged clothing. It is said that they are to be quartered in the town. Now even the undecided population is determined not to abandon their homes.

In the midst of the excitement a new rumor: Waxweiler will be forcibly evacuated. Indeed, that is the plan for the whole area from the border to the Prüm river. I can't believe it. The thought of abandoning my home with all the household goods, books, etc. does not sit well with me. So I explain to the Ortsgruppenleiter, whom I found in the street, that I will not leave at any cost. I am firm, I am determined to stay. "And if commanded from above?" "Not even then," is my answer. "Then you will have to take the consequences!" "I do," I reply.

A short time later, the forced evacuation is ordered. The regional Nazi leader, Gauamtsleiter Bang of Koblenz is the author of this measure. The Ortsgruppenleiter had signed the order: within one hour, the entire population with hand luggage and food enough for 48 hours is to depart for the Kyll river (about 20 km East). It's clear to me that the Politicians are playing games with the population. That's why I am determined to use all of my means to thwart the forced evacuation.

To emphasize the order, it says: "Whoever does not obey the order, is regarded as sympathizing with the enemy and has to bear the consequences." I first begin to publicly protest against this particular phrase, and almost everyone there agrees. Then I declare that I will not leave the town, and I advise everyone to do the same. I explain that they are refusing to grant us speedy liberation by the advancing American Military. If I had to go, I would go towards the Americans, not backwards or even across the Rhine river. Many women are crying and questions come from the village: "Pastor, what should we do?" My advice is the same to all, "Do not leave under any circumstances."

In the midst of the turmoil, a military car drives through the town. It is a German General. The crowd stops the car and some women express their concerns to the general, "What are we going to do?" The General replies, "Stay here, no matter what. The streets are already blocked by supply trucks. Now they are sending civilians into these urgently needed supply routes." In my opinion this answer helps a lot. Towards evening everyone is determined to stay. Our first victory over the Nazi party has been won. Who would blame us for celebrating this "victory" in a small circle with a bottle of wine and going to bed that night with the indescribable feeling of still having a home!

September 17, 1944

Yesterday, unlike the previous day, was peacefully quiet. Now I seriously ask myself several times: "Did this really happen, or were you just having a nightmare?" On Saturday afternoon I am pretty busy in the confessional, as a result of the events of the last few days. For today, the bishop ordered a day of prayer and repentance.

During the night, I am awakened several times by the dull thud of shells in a distance, but I fall asleep again and again. Only when I open the bedroom window in the morning, do I clearly hear the sound that was so familiar to me from World War 1, the shriek of shelling.

The impacts cannot be too far away. What to do? Is it advisable to hold the service in the completely unprotected church? But around 7 o'clock the artillery fire falls silent. During the homily of the Mass I reassure the believers and tell them to stay in their homes during the day. To keep the people safe in their homes I blow off the all-day prayer service. If nothing special happens during the daytime, we will have a service of repentance at 7 PM. It stays calm. A soft, melancholy rain trickles down all day. The mood is further depressed by the cloudy weather. What will happen? The shelling of the previous night had happened in the neighboring town of Lünebach, an hour away. My church branch in Heilhausen is half-way between Lünebach and Waxweiler. In the morning I ask a few congregants from Heilhausen if they are afraid, but they didn't hear any shooting.

October 2, 1944

We are still hoping for immediate rescue through the onward movement of the Americans. In recent days, more and more German troops march through the town towards the war front on their way to the bunker line. The mood of the troops is varied. A sergeant confidently hopes that the new weapon promised by the Führer will soon cause a total turnaround. We got used to the shelling around the outskirts of town. The town itself has been spared so far; only the train station got hit a few nights ago. Some other impacts went into fields. Except for some shattered window panes there's been no damage. But for the last few days some strange vehicles have come through town. Farm wagons loaded with feed, household goods, and bedding, pull through town in ever-larger columns. They come from the border villages, where it's gradually becoming intolerable because of ever-increasing artillery fire. It's a pathetic scene, especially with the incessant rain. The sight of this pitiful procession of fleeing people depresses our mood. After all, will the horrors of the wandering warfare finally drive us out of our town? Since the beginning of September we pray the Rosary every evening in church. Quite a number of women, men, youth and children come. The prayer for protection of our homes becomes ever more urgent and imploring.

During the evening, at 8:30 PM, a peculiar hiss passes over the town. A shell? We don't hear any impact. Maybe a decoy, we hope. After a while the conversation starts to flow again. At 9:30 pm, exactly one hour after the peculiar sound, we hear a whistling and hissing and then a violent detonation. The lights go out for a moment. The first impact in town. We rush outside immediately. The impact is very close to the church, in a stable. You can't see a thing because of the smoke and dust, but the damage doesn't seem so bad. The certainty is paralyzing that now the town lies in the impact area of enemy artillery. When will the next shell come?

I'm troubled for the coming night. In any case, we will set up our cots on the ground floor instead of the second floor. At 10:30PM, the next impact hits. Through the window I see thick smoke billowing past the west side of the church. So again it hit near the church. If this goes on, I have little hope that the church will be whole by morning. Then we go to sleep. Regularly every hour a shell lands in the town, more or less close to the church. What's that supposed to mean? Between the impacts I fall asleep again and again to be awakened by every new detonation. Towards morning it quiets down. My first walk after getting up is to church. A house near the church is hit on the roof. The house had been vacant for two days. Strangely enough, the church has remained intact. Only one of the choir area windows has a small hole. Later I find a small piece of shrapnel in the inside.

October 3, 1944

The day has been quiet. Of course, in the morning, everyone is worried, but nobody has been hurt. With anxious concern we wait for evening. Is the shooting going to happen again? As darkness falls, the streets are deserted. The night is quiet.

October 9, 1944

The bombardment of the town has not been repeated. We do hear impacts of shells night after night, but the town itself is spared, so we get used to it and make nothing more of it. Meanwhile, several hundred combat engineers have arrived from the city of Trier. Since they have to work on Sundays, the men ask to have a church service in the evening. I want to grant their wish. The first evening service turns out to be a moving experience. In the morning our regular worship service is held for the faithful of the parish, in the evening the church is reserved for the combat engineers. Approximately one thousand men fill the church. As I approach the altar, I hear the song from these thousand male voices: "Hier liegt vor deiner Majestät." (See Appendix for translated lyrics)

The powerful singing touches our hearts deeply. Year after year since the beginning of the war the male population in our churches has dwindled. We are not used to such powerful worship anymore. I am touched to the depths of my heart. I can sense that others have the same experience. For many these evening services are the only relief from the daily monotony, the unfamiliar life with its hard physical labor, sparse food, primitive accommodations and harassing treatment by the Nazi officials. Many have found their way back to church, which they had not cared about in better times.

October 16, 1944

The refugee arrivals continue. Yes, they are still increasing every day. The so-called red border zone is now officially vacated. People are barely able to survive in their villages. Many have lost their lives trying to recover their belongings. Others have been more or less seriously wounded. Since October 4, Lünebach, our neighboring parish, has been officially evacuated by nearly all civilians. A few people remain in their homes and cellars. More than the shells, they fear the SS evacuation commands.

October 17, 1944

This afternoon I am kindly asked to come to the hospital. A military transport brought in a boy of only about seven and his mother. They are from Lünebach. Both were wounded by a shell. The boy, lying on a stretcher, is completely wrapped up in bandages, through which the blood already permeates; the exposed face is covered with blood and dirt. The little boy keeps calling for his mother, who is on a nearby stretcher with bandaged limbs. She is bloody and trembling with fear. The mother tells how it happened. She had not been able to make the decision to leave their home and so they stayed behind with others. She was just about to fetch water at the river Prüm. There had not been any shooting for a few hours, but then, an explosion. She sees a bright flash of light and immediately the boy screams and crumples to the ground covered in blood. I give the last rights to the boy. In his brief moments of consciousness, I can't speak coherently with the child or do more for him, but miraculously the boy lives, and in the evening, mother and child are taken to the nearby troop headquarters for treatment. After the first treatment, the wounded civilians are transferred by the military to hospitals farther inland. Almost every day wounded civilians arrive together with the wounded soldiers.

November 1, 1944

All Saints Day!

We got used to being on the front line, to the constant shooting and the exploding shells. As a precaution we do not do the traditional procession to the cemetery with the whole congregation. It's not easy to move through the tremendous traffic on the roads. I'm postponing the blessing of the graves until All Souls' Day after the early morning service.

November 5, 1944

Since nothing seems to be changing in our day-to-day situation, I've started having regular religious education classes again. The children like to come together. They are

glad to get lessons again. School has been closed since
August. During our lessons, the constant boom of shell strikes
doesn't bother us anymore, unless a shell lands close by. I also
visit my branch churches again, two of which have already
been under fire.

November 12, 1944

Almost every day fellow priests from the border parishes visit
me. They use my rectory as a stopover on their way back to
their vacated parishes, to visit with the few remaining church
members and to recover contents from their households.

Most of them have settled in places farther East from the
border, where many of their parishioners are housed
temporarily. These trips towards the front are not without
danger, because the roads are almost constantly under fire.
Some of them make great sacrifices and joyfully bear great
privations and the hardships of evacuation with their
parishioners.

November 13, 1944

Six men from the combat engineer brass have been billeted in
my rectory for six weeks. I cleared out my former living room
to accommodate them. Again and again passing troops ask for
quarters. Often, just about every free corner in the house is
occupied. My relatives now often share space with a family
from bomb-damaged Hagen, who lives in the parish hall.
Months ago we made an emergency apartment in the cellar of
the hall. We put several cots there. It looks quite comfortable
and they seem to sleep soundly in spite of the constant shell
strikes.

December 1, 1944

For several weeks we have had brisk military traffic coming through town. Again and again new Wehrmacht troops move to the Westwall. A divisional staff is to billeted here soon. For the first time since the catastrophic retreat in September, the front lines will again have organized German military. There are rumors of impending military operations in our front sector. Since September we are practically cut off from the outside world. The mail comes only sporadically, and it must be picked up by couriers from the nearby town of Schönecken. Those who want to "travel" can only do so if they are taken by military vehicles. To this end, passengers stand at the "hitchhiker station" at the Kanal, the intersection in the lower village. They let the military police know that they need a ride, and they stop a car. In this way people can then reach public transportation further inland.

December 12, 1944

It's an open secret that a German offensive will start shortly. We are still doubtful about the truth of this rumor, for the lack of essential military necessities is too obvious, but the feverish activity of the military commanders can have no other purpose. Some revel in bold dreams again. The thoughtless are already talking about our troops soon being back at the Kanal. The more insightful think: Yes, but as prisoners.

December 15, 1944

Everything is tense, the offensive may start any day. More and more troops are moving forward. We are comforted by the thought that we will then come out of the range of enemy artillery again. The refugees are hoping for a speedy return to their partly destroyed towns.

December 16, 1944

It has become a fact. Since early this morning around five o'clock we hear the dull thunder of gunfire from the border. And between 5 and 6 o'clock it has increased to a barrage. The military staff and most of the troops left during the night. More and more troops are moving forward. In the evening, the sounds of detonation disappear, a sign that the offensive has had an initial success.

December 17, 1944

Sunday. For days now the evacuated pastor of Lünebach and his sister live with me in the rectory. They hope to return to his parish after the troops advance. After the rainy weather of the last few days, the sky clears up today for the first time. At about 10 o'clock the sun shines down from a blue sky. We had not seen any enemy planes for the last week, but as soon as it clears up the skies become alive. The German deployment took place without disruption under the protection of the overcast sky. Now the sky is suddenly teeming with hostile fighter bombers. The anti-aircraft guns stationed around all the surrounding hills suddenly start up. It's a hell of a spectacle, compounded by the rumble of tanks rolling in endless chains through the town towards the Western Front. The roads to the front are completely closed to civilians now. Only under mortal danger can one pass by the tanks, which roll incessantly forward. The mud in the streets is now churned almost three feet deep. It's like a swamp. When I arrive home after the main church service, the mayor appears. He is very tense and prohibits any church service during the day from now on because of the danger to the population. We wonder where all these war materials, tanks, vehicles and the massive amounts of gasoline have come from. It seemed in the past few weeks as if we had nothing left. They've probably scraped together all the remaining stock from all over Germany.

December 18, 1944

Some amazing rumors are floating around: Liège in Belgium has fallen to the Germans. Others claim to know that we have already driven a wedge as far as Antwerp. The expressions of returning wounded soldiers betray nothing of the sort. We suspended the regular religious education classes again last week, but Christmas preparations begin in the church. The children, under the guidance of an eager volunteer, rehearsed some Advent and Christmas plays, which we perform in front of the individual groups in the sacristy - our room for religion classes. The room is festively decorated with pine greenery. Since the beginning of Advent the fragrant Advent wreath hangs in the room. In the hope of continuing lessons after the holidays, I give the children a short Christmas vacation.

December 20, 1944

Today during the late afternoon, the head of the Office of the Ministry of Economic Affairs comes to me, with an officer, and demands that the church be used as overnight accommodation for a thousand captured American soldiers. Of course I resist. We go through all the accommodation options. There is no other option, since well over a thousand combat engineers - domestic and foreign – are already quartered in private homes in the town. So as not to let the POWs spend the night outdoors, I finally give in. After placing the Blessed Sacrament into the sacristy, I release the church to the officer. Towards evening the transport arrives. The guards assure us that they will take care there is utmost order and cleanliness. Nine hundred men are then housed in the church. The church is completely filled; our huge nativity scene takes up space under the organ gallery, so the pews fill up fast. The remaining soldiers bed down on the floor.

December 21, 1944

I am at the church early this morning. The POWs have already left the church and are milling around outside. Shortly afterwards they move away. I decided to move the church service to the hospital chapel, a 5-minute walk away.

When I return afterwards, the floor of the church is swept clean, but thick dust is on everything. In this condition, the church cannot be used for Christmas services. I call together about a dozen girls. They scrub and clean all day and in the evening the church is again spotless.

December 24, 1944

Sunday, Christmas Eve. On top of accommodating the combat engineers, I got orders to billet more: a general judge. Again a divisional headquarters is accommodated in the town. When I come to the church early this morning, a squad of combat engineers is standing in front of the church with two female Red Cross helpers. They had marched through the night and today they are supposed to cross the border and mend the roads that were badly damaged by the advance. It's freezing cold out. They ask to rest in the church. I let them in. The cold, unheated church seems warm to them. They sit in the back pews and soon fall asleep. I send the two Red Cross girls to the rectory. In the afternoon I have a lot of work in the confessional. I hear the buzzing of enemy bomber formations overhead and then powerful detonations in the distance. Later we learn that the neighboring town of Lünebach has been hit again and is now almost completely destroyed. It's a blessing that the town had been vacated by the population months ago. But there are still many civilian contractors there. Hundreds of them are said to be buried under the rubble. This is how the 6th war Christmas begins. At home in the evening we celebrate a traditional Christmas Eve with my neighboring colleague and his sister. Suddenly the doorbell rings. A soldier is standing outside. He has been on the way to the front for days and asks for a night's lodging. It is Christmas Eve, that's why we invite him in, although all rooms are occupied. We let him take part in our household celebration and give him a plate of cookies. The boy is grateful. After a while he says, "If my parents knew how beautifully I am celebrating Christmas, they sure would be happy." We find out he is from the Hanover area. The next day he has to join his troop early in the morning. We go to bed after my colleague holds the midnight mass in the hospital. Everything is peaceful and quiet outside. No sound disturbs the peace of the Holy Night. At least on the night of the dearest of all celebrations the better in man has triumphed over all predatory instincts! After all, it seems the tender breath of the festival of love has covered our murderous world and has pierced, if only for a moment, the ice-cold crust of hatred.

December 25, 1944

It's the 6th Christmas during wartime! I hold the first Christmas mass at 5:00AM, like every other year. On my way to church I already hear suspicious aircraft noises. Well blacked-out towards the outside, the church shines bright with festive lights inside. During the church service again and again we hear the howling engine noise of a circulating Jabo (short for Jagdbomber, hunter-bomber). In the silence during the transubstantiation the siren-like sound of the diving Jabo is downright sinister. I hurry to finish the transubstantiation. After this we hold a silent Mass, but suddenly the power goes out. The regular Christmas service cannot be held until the evening. We've lost power often in the last few months, but it usually came right back on. So we hope this time it will, too. But even in the evening there was no electricity. The most disorienting thing about it is that we can't listen to the radio news. So we are now completely cut off from the outside world. Newspapers have not been delivered for weeks.

December 26, 1944

The holidays are over and done with and everyday life is back. The sounds in the sky get more and more scary every day. The bomber formations, which fly over us more and more, don't bother us. We feel pretty safe from them. Dangerous are the Jabos with their nerve-wracking noises. Nevertheless, we have not sheltered in the cellar in recent days. At most, we watch them go around and listen for the bombs falling at some distance, mostly on the access roads to the front. Supplying the German troops is becoming increasingly difficult. All traffic stops on clear days. As soon as dusk settles, the roads come to life again.

So it is understandable that the high expectations so many had of the current campaign, have long since yielded to a deeply pessimistic mood. The reports from the troops coming from the front confirm our assumptions: The offensive - we only call it the raid - has stalled. What we realists have known for a long time, the "stalwarts" gradually begin to understand. The war is lost. This crazy offensive campaign has only uselessly prolonged the incalculable devastation of our border zone, not to mention the loss of life. They are talking of huge losses in the battle for Bastogne. The Wehrmacht wanted to take Bastogne without additional artillery supply, because there were supposed to be tremendous amounts of war supplies stored there. Now we hear that German troops are trapped there. In my house, the number of people being billeted still grows almost every day.

December 29, 1944

This afternoon, the pastor from the Lünebach wants to return to his town. We have just settled down for lunch, when another Jabo - or even several - howl over us. The howling becomes more and more uncanny. We decide to go to the cellar, because it sounds like the guy in the air will attack soon. In a hurry, we go to the cellar. I'm still standing in the front door when he's already whooshing over us, an explosion and then hot air strikes me; I stooped involuntarily and as I straighten up again I see smoke and flames in the house next door. "Fire," I scream into the cellar and run into the street to raise the alarm. Most people, like us, had gone into their cellars. We fear the spread of fire to the rectory. That's why we move at least the bedding out of the upper floors. That's how we learned that something must have happened with the rectory. The inner wall of my bedroom is bulged in about 3 feet. Quickly we check the next room. What a mess. The rather thick outer wall has a man-sized hole. The furniture is totally destroyed. The whole room is full of stones and dust. In the wall opening we find the battered and tattered remains of a gasoline container, the reserve tank for the air plane. A devastating effect, but fortunately the canister did not explode, as in the neighboring house. Otherwise all would have burned before we noticed. With a glance I assess the situation; for the time being there's nothing we can do here. We run over to the neighboring house, where our helping hands are needed more. As I step into the street, the first thing I notice is the truck bearing the symbol of the SS. It faces our house. The cargo: gasoline barrels. The white tin barrels flash bright in the brilliant winter sun; what a great target for a Jabo. From now on we will no longer permit Wehrmacht vehicles to park within the town limits. The behavior of the SS drivers is downright criminally reckless. After a few hours, the fire at the neighbor's house is extinguished. A number of rooms and the staircase are burned out. In the evening I also look at the ruins in my house again. And so the first fighter damage in the town hit the rectory. The partial loss of my furnishings doesn't bother me that much. We will have to reckon with worse. The day has brought one good thing: We are now more careful. In the future we will look for better shelter as soon as we hear the approach of the dangerous Jabos.

December 31, 1944

New Year's Eve. The year 1944, which has been so eventful especially in its second half, comes to an end. Since it's Sunday, I hold the regular church service at night as sort of an end-of-year mass. Uninterrupted Jabo noise is in the air until dark. I have to hurry the church service, but I need to give a short sermon. At this important time, I cannot let New Year's Eve pass by without a few words. So I hold a brief review with my parish. Despite all the hardships of the last months, God has protected and sustained us. Above all, we have kept our homes. That's why the hymn "Te Deum laudeamus" is so appropriate tonight (see appendix for lyrics). Just a short revelation: Dark as never before are the days and weeks ahead of us, but in all our effort we have confidence. With the "Te Deum" and the blessing of the Lord, we close the most solemn and sincere year-end service.

January 1, 1945

As always lately, if I sleep upstairs, I don't fully undress. I am awakened at 1:30AM by the spectacular noise caused by a Jabo. Several times before I had woken up a bit from the same noise, but fell asleep again. This time however, the pilot is raging in the air. He comes back every half hour. As often as he flies over the town, he fires his onboard weapon like crazy.

My sister comes to wake me with the message that once again a Wehrmacht vehicle is parked in front of our house. Since the frenzy happened last Friday, we hate the Wehrmacht vehicles being parked in the street. I get up immediately and go outside. Sure enough, right in front of the entrance to the rectory, in the bright moonlight, stands a military truck. No driver is to be found. Anyway, it's dead quiet on the streets. The full moon stands quietly in the sky and sends its ghostly light from the starry sky over the town. The shadows of houses are like deep black squares in the day-bright streets. I sound the alarm. Two guys come running out of a side street to the truck. The drivers. I yell at them and tell them to drive the truck out of town immediately. After several crude exchanges, they start the truck and drive off. I lie down again. At 5:00AM a powerful explosion wakes me up. Now the guy has dumped a bomb. It must be very close. Again my sister comes, she does not want me to stay upstairs.

So I settle down on the ground floor. At 7:00AM I am awakened by a new roar. It seems to me that all the cabinets in the room have fallen over. Also, I hear glass shattering endlessly. I jump up: in the room everything is in its usual place. Only broken glass is on the floor; some window panes fell into the room. The bomb must have fallen into the yard, or at least into the garden. I run out, go around the house: nothing to see. Funny! Then I dress and go to church to hold the morning mass. As I leave the house I see the neighbors of the church run towards me, bundles of clothes on their shoulders. Excited, they yell at me: "At the church, all the windows are broken, go look." Right! On the west side of the church gape empty window openings. The pavement is covered with glass. In tangled shreds the stained-glass windows and their led coating hang from the openings. Through the empty window openings, the frosty cold of the 1st of January penetrates. I cancel the service for today and hold a silent Holy Mass in the hospital chapel.

January 5, 1945

The bombs on New Year's Eve and New Year's Day had all fallen in close proximity to the church. Thank God, no damage has been done except for the broken windows. The beginning of the year was not auspicious. During the blizzards of recent days, the floor and the pews of the church were covered with a 12-inch layer of snow far into the interior. Add to that the freezing cold. So we cannot hold a service there. I have been holding all church services in the hospital chapel, but tomorrow is a holiday, and I really need the big church to accommodate all the parishioners. With an vast amount of effort, I succeed in getting leftover boards from the barracks and the help of a carpenter, who, with a few boys, boards up the windows.

January 6, 1945

It was barely tolerable during the morning Mass. In the church the temperature was minus 8° Celsius (17°Fahrenheit). I have to make sure that the services do not last too long. I plan on a quiet Masses, without preaching, with at most a heartfelt word on the current times following the liturgy. The holy water is frozen and so is the water in the ablution container. Luckily, I can still heat the sacristy, which has remained intact until now. So at least I have a warm room for holding confession. We now have to visit our cellar shelter more often every day. Rarely can we eat without interruption by the Jabos. Bombs fall around the town almost every day, and so it is again this afternoon. As a result, the shockwaves have busted out all of the boarded up church windows again. Now we have to do the work all over again. It gets quieter after dark. So we can at least sit together in the evening with a little more comfort and discuss the situation. The electricity has not come back on. We make do with whatever we have, because there is a lack of candles and kerosene. So during the day we salvage the remaining wax and make little lights, so we don't have to sit in the dark during the winter evenings. Most evenings, neighbors come together, so time passes faster and you save light.

January 8, 1945

All the larger towns on the Prüm river have been the target of heavy bombing and are more or less in ruins. Incomprehensibly Waxweiler has been spared until now. We know that one day it will be our turn. Of course we hope that won't be the case.

That today our town should become the target of a serious attack, nobody imagined. The clear frosty weather is replaced by a light thaw. The sky is completely overcast. At 9:00AM a light snowfall sets in. Nobody anticipates airplanes flying in this weather. And indeed, the sky is peacefully silent. At 10:30AM the hum of heavy bombers is heard. Bomber formations don't usually harm us. Life on the street continues, as always with such overflights, but now the hum grows louder. The bombers turn around just beyond the town.

Suddenly, there is a sign of attack, a white smoke trail over the town, and the first bombs are already fizzing and crackling. Everyone flees and seeks cover. I also dash into the basement when the first bombs crash so close. And now it's like a hurricane over us. The cellar trembles and shakes at the impacts; it's getting closer - here comes the roar. For a few minutes we believe our last moment has come. Then suddenly there's silence. I immediately grab the anointing oil and rush into the street. The first people are already walking there, excitedly calling out the street names where the bombs fell. I hear of one house that's completely obliterated. I estimate that I heard about 200 impacts. I run to the first crash site. Luckily, it looks like most of the bombs fell outside of town. Only the southern part of the town was strafed in its full width and that's where the destruction is. In fact, a large two-story house has completely disappeared; only a desolate pile of stones still hints at the place where it stood. Approximately a dozen people, men, women and adolescents are already in the process of recovering the residents, who are thought to be still alive under the rubble. They have not yet reached the cellar. I make the sign of the cross and whisper the words of absolution over the rubble, then hurry on to other rubble heaps. An even larger number of people is suspected to have taken cover in the cellar of the half-destroyed building of the district court. Here, it would be mainly soldiers and workers. A high heap of rubble lies above the cellar; some foreign workers – Polish men are hacking their way through. A house-sized crater gapes in the middle of the street in front of the barracks beyond the bridge. The first stretchers bearing the dead are arriving from the destroyed barracks. There are no survivors left in that area. Wounded people have already been taken to the hospital. There are only dead people over there. So I run to the hospital. The cellar is packed with the injured. All the wounded are soldiers who are already wearing bandages. No one is mortally wounded, so I run back to the first accident site to see if anyone has been recovered in the meantime. As I get on the road, again engine noise. In agitated haste soldiers and civilians run back and forth. Nobody wants to go into the cellars. Everyone runs out of town. Children cry for their mothers. The place where everyone is going was just under the last bombing. I run to the ruined house; they have not found anyone yet. Neighbors say that the house did not have a real cellar at all. Then no one is alive anymore from those who were inside. A soldier discovers two corpses about 50 steps from the house. They are completely covered in rubble, only the hair that protrudes slightly has made the discovery possible. We uncover the bodies: They are two daughters of the same family. The one was married and had two children. She is terribly mutilated. From there we cautiously dig towards the house and discover four children, one after the other, then the mother and finally, after a long search, the severed head of the father. The son-in-law is missing, the husband of the daughter first discovered and a daughter-in-law. On the whole, 10 people died in one house. Meanwhile, in the mortuary of the hospital, the bodies of 5 young women have been brought. They, too, died in the barracks on the other side of the bridge. There is no visible damage to their bodies. So they died because of the air pressure. These girls are all from a Mosel village who had been in the forced labor troop here. They had arrived just the evening before. In the afternoon of this eventfully misfortunate day, families are seen leaving the town in droves and moving into the more sheltered, less endangered villages, which are remote from the main roads. It's clear to us that the bomb attack on our town happened because we are considered the major thoroughfare to the front. With bedding and clothes packed on small hand carts the people, mostly women and children, move out. Towards evening the town is deserted. What will be next?

January 9, 1945

Last night a young woman came to me. She is worried about the fate of three wounded relatives: husband, mother-in-law and her niece. The niece is the daughter of her sister who had evacuated to Thuringia. The three had left their house in the morning during the bombing raid in order to escape to a farm about 20 minutes away where they had spent some days previously. They have not returned yet. Inquiries have revealed that yesterday they were not at their usual refuge at all. However, about the time they had left the house, a bomb hit 60 steps away and covered the spot with a mountain of dirt and blocked the road they had to pass. Could they be buried under the dirt! In the afternoon, the road which is a much-used supply road to the war front, is cleared, so that the traffic can flow again. No trace has been discovered of the missing people, though. The next morning the salvage work continues; it is almost certain now that they are under the dirt. At 10:00AM I head over to the site. The man's boots and the heavily dented rear wheel of a bicycle have just been uncovered. So the speculations had come true. In addition to the three above, another 20-year-old neighbor was recovered. All were terribly disfigured, and of course dead. Thus, the death toll of yesterday's air raid is 14 parishioners. The exact number of the others who have perished cannot be determined. This afternoon, the first evacuees came home again. Apparently the living conditions in the other villages are not at all comfortable. After the first fright is over, calm returns.

January 15, 1945

Very early this morning, with great participation by the town, we buried the victims of Monday's air raid in a common grave. There are a total of 24 victims: 14 parishioners, 5 young women from the forced labor camp, and the others were foreign workers. We do not have enough wood left in town to make coffins for everyone. So we have to bury over half of the dead without.

We have to do the funeral very early in the morning, because as soon as it's daylight the Jabos dominate the airspace with their engine growls and the roads with bombs and guns. As with the other funerals, which I do almost daily now, we have to choose the early morning hours. Today it's cloudy with rain. A depressed mood is above all involved. Almost every day brings new surprises. Everyone restlessly rushes along to avoid the Jabos. We can only do the bare necessities as we wait for more attacks from the air. It gets quiet around 5 in the afternoon. Then it's time to fix the smashed windows from the day. Whenever we take refuge in the cellar, about a dozen times a day, we first quickly open the windows in the house so that the explosions don't shatter all the glass. Of course, now it is always cold in the house.

In addition, the news reports from the front become increasingly grave. The first enemy shells fly over us since the beginning of the recent offensive. More than all of the news reports, this causes us to suspect the true state of affairs. The rumbling of the guns gets closer every day. Almost uninterruptedly we hear the impacts of shells. Soldiers are constantly dragging through the town. Those who can still walk are sick and wounded. Everyone looks very run-down, torn-up, with worn-out uniforms, some with awful footwear in this wet, cold weather. Everyone is hungry and begs for food; Ravenously, they bite into the bit of dry bread that we give them. Food deliveries are almost non-existent, as every delivery near the front is deadly dangerous. For days there is no bread at the bakery – because they currently have no flour and no firewood. Those who did not store provisions last fall are in dire straits now.

A group of brave men went to the border villages to find if there was anything left over by the Wehrmacht and possibly grain left behind by the civilian population. The success was meager. We console ourselves that this cannot go on much longer, otherwise none of us will survive. Even the most hopeful optimist now sees that the war is lost. "Why don't the Nazi criminals give up?" Is not only asked by civilians, but by almost every soldier.

January 18, 1945

Since the beginning of the heavy bombing of the town, whole families spend their days in small earth bunkers, most of which are located on the slope of a side valley of the Prüm river. These earth bunkers were built last fall by the population. Several families did this work together and built them as protection from artillery fire when the front would move through.

The bunkers aren't even completely safe against shells, let alone bombs, but they are outside of town, off the road, and so they at least give people a slight feeling of security. I visit two of the bunkers today. Difficult climbing paths lead to a dark hole in the ground. Inside, the bunker is like a cave, just barely high enough to sit on a bench that runs along the earth walls. On this bench 9-12 people sit closely together, mostly women and girls. In the middle is a small stove. The entrance is covered by a blanket that keeps in the heat. No lights burn during the day, so that you can't see a thing when you first enter the dark. After some time, your eyes get used to the twilight; then you see tolerably well, because some light penetrates through a small gap near the ceiling at the entrance. Some of the women are completely exhausted and at their wits end. The slightest motor noise excites them, they start shaking and crying. What will happen to them if this continues? Sure, no one is comfortable with the daily bombing around town. Since the heavy attack, my rectory cellar, although it is below earth level and arched, seems no longer safe enough. In case of danger, we go to the cellar of the neighboring house, which is well supported and roomier. Nearly 20-30 people are gathered there nightly. Even though the cellar is crowded, it is better than staying in the musty earth bunkers from day to day.

January 22, 1945

The front is getting closer again. A few weeks ago a field hospital of the SS was established in one of our branch churches, and the small chapel was occupied by the wounded. This field hospital has now been moved back inland and replaced by a casualty clearing station. Also in the neighboring parish Ringhuscheid a casualty clearing station was started. The village has been declared a hospital village, that is to say, it should no longer be the target of enemy bombing and artillery attacks. We only hope to be so lucky in Waxweiler. How nice that would be! It would be like paradise if we no longer had to constantly be on the watch for Jabos; no longer constantly had to chase back and forth between work and shelter like hunted game; to be safe from the treacherous artillery raids. For days it's been rumored that our town would indeed become a casualty clearing station. This time the rumors have been confirmed. Since Saturday the flags of the Red Cross are flying from the church steeple. The clearing stations of two troop units have recognized our town as their location. We willingly provide all available rooms for the teams and their patients. Life returns to the town. Street traffic returns to normal. One sees the relief on the faces of the passers-by, the consciousness of being protected from all the peril of the last weeks. Three military chaplains are quartered with me. I am happy to accommodate them. Although each of the three brothers is characteristically different, we understand each other well. For the first few days, we talked a lot about our enemies' respect for the "Red Cross." In the beginning of the invasion, the Red Cross gave absolute protection, but all the abuses that our troops or the SS had done under the guise of the Red Cross, has influenced the behavior of our enemy.

Various events, especially those of the last few weeks, make it impossible to have a feeling of complete security. These observations also dampen our confidence, but this morning I decided to visit my neighboring church branches once more. I longed to move beyond the borders of the town. Since Christmas, I had not visited them, as military chaplains were stationed in both chapel towns, and they were willing to accept the civilian population too. The constant presence of Jabos in recent weeks made any hike to neighboring villages deadly dangerous. Now I counted on the protection of the Red Cross. About 10:00AM I started on my way. The weather was hazy, which also had a calming effect. It is only when I start climbing the hill outside of town that I realize the snow is knee-deep. Should I turn back? Oh well, it will be fine.

After about 15 minutes the sky clears. Immediately I hear the buzzing in the air: the first Jabo squadron! From high up on my footpath along the mountain, I notice civilian workers scattering sand on the snow-covered road down in the valley. They look like so many black dots against the snowy road. In between were long lines of people, one behind the other, dragging their luggage on small homemade wooden sleds. I start getting nervous.

Now that the sun is breaking through, the Jabos start circling above me. I take cover near a hedge, because being a lone black dot on a snow-white surface is dangerous, but without any shooting, the Jabos disappear after a few minutes. I continue on my way. It is infinitely laborious to wade through the knee-deep snow. I am within 50 steps of the village of Bellscheid, which I have to pass to get to my destination, when another fierce engine noise starts up. Then suddenly the usual siren-like, nerve-wrenching howl of a Jabo dive. Breathlessly I hurry the last three steps to the next tree. I throw myself into the snow and the first shell rushes past me. I heard a tremendous explosion and the whirring of splinters. And now for hours there follows a truly hellish howling, rushing, crackling and whirring. I give up all hope of getting out of this scary situation alive. I know the attacks were aimed at the road below, but the shells fall so frighteningly close to me that I fear, at any moment, I will be the victim of this murderous chaos. Finally, deafening gunfire starts up. The planes must fly at the lowest altitude possible because I feel them right above me. Finally, after an eternity, the noise ebbs away. The planes are leaving. Only when it is complete silent I carefully raise my head. My body made a foxhole in the snow. The previously glaring white area around me is black and covered in innumerable charred shrapnel. I hurry to the next house without looking back. If the attack resumes, at least I will be under cover and with other people. Folks were just about to sweep away the broken glass from the window sills. They could scarcely believe that I had been outside during the attack and survived it. After a short rest I hurry to Ringhuscheid. At 2:00PM another humming of the Jabos. At first we don't let them disturb our conversation, but then it gets too scary for me. I'm still shaken from my experience that morning, so that I'm the only one taking refuge in the cellar.

But nothing more happens. We hear the flights over Waxweiler during the afternoon. I decide to stay in Ringhuscheid. Then - in the middle of our conversation –2 or 3 terrible explosions happen nearby and the splinters fall on the roof of the barn near us. We hurry into the cellar. A soldier comes rushing into the house and screams, "The church is hit." We rush out of the cellar into the Ringhuscheid church, where a huge hole greets us. In the church are stones, rubble and dust an inch thick. After that, I head straight for home to Waxweiler. When I pass the hedge where I had first sought protection from the Jabos in the morning, everything is black and charred. About a dozen bomb craters lay all around the hedge. A chill trickles down my spine when I see that. As I approach Waxweiler, people come towards me dragging handcarts, loaded with bundles. They want to flee to Niederpierscheid, a small village nearby. In Waxweiler the planes had been bad again in the afternoon. Some houses were obliterated, others were damaged. The church was also hit. A bomb, judging by the crater a very heavy caliber, had actually fallen near the church. Now the windows on the street side were all shattered.

The frames of the already damaged and boarded up windows, are once again busted out by the bombs after only one or two days. Now empty windows are gaping all around the church. During the week we hold mass in the hospital chapel, but on Sunday we submit to the weather conditions. When the wind blows wildly, the altarpieces and my robes flutter around my head. I hold the ablution cover over the chalice with the host so that the storm doesn't blow the communion away. But we had not a single human casualty in the attack of the day; the one house that was completely destroyed had already been abandoned for days, and the bomb that destroyed the stained glass windows in the church fell a distance away from a building that housed some seriously wounded people.

In spite of all protests, the town officials do not succeed in getting a troop of combat engineers, who billeted in the cellar of this building, to move out. Because of our hospital status this is a violation of the Geneva Convention. At midday during the flyovers the combat engineers were even working outdoors. No wonder our enemies do not respect the Red Cross flag.

January 28, 1945

This week, a divisional pastor is lodging with me. The war front has been moved back and the church has established a third hub here. For days now, the town has been in enemy artillery reach again and rumor has it that all First Aid stations will move back as well. All roads outside of town are scarred with shell craters already. The town itself hasn't had any new impacts yet. A few days ago I buried a French woman at the request of the French forced laborers, who are working on entrenchments in the town. They found her, completely charred, among the ruins of the youth center, which had burned to the ground during the heavy attack of the 8th of January.

4 February 1945

The First Aid stations have been completely relocated during the week. We hear that the Americans are once again fighting all along the nearby Westwall. Shells frequently hiss over the town. All access roads are being pummeled with artillery volleys. Visiting Sunday mass is already quite dangerous for the pastors of the outlying chapels. Nevertheless, besides children, the adults are still faithful to come to church. Those vehicles and crews that move backward from the front through our town look run-down now. Many of the trucks run so poorly that they have to be pushed up the small rise in front of the rectory.

A flak column, retreating from the front, has been positioned to the hills south of the town. They were completely out of fuel, and 16 soldiers harnessed themselves in front of the guns and pulled them up the mountain. They were singing morbid songs. Most soldiers are completely ragged and very hungry. Some of them have been out of food for days, because supplies cannot move forward due to the air surveillance by the enemy. Hopefully that indicates the end of the war for us. If only it would come, and soon! Today, some German tanks rolled through the street, what a miserable sight. They were so worn out that they had to stop about every 30 feet until the engine could cool down a bit. Only then could they get on with it at all. My rectory is now vacant of military for the first time since the beginning of September last year. The last entrenchers have pulled out, and we don't know whether the entrenchments around town are now ready to fight or not. A number of troop squads are still billeted in some of the homes. For weeks they have been wandering around town. Nobody knows what they're up to. Their camouflaged vehicles are parked in alleys all around town. When asked, they say they have to wait for fuel and that their vehicles have to be repaired, and that the necessary spare parts are still missing. In reality, these people seem to have no connection with their units anymore. It's the beginning of the end.

February 11, 1945

All organized German Military is gone from the town. Waxweiler itself presents a quiet, peaceful picture. Only the explosions of nearby shells remind us that there's a war going on. The front must be very close. We do not hear anything for certain. The reports from passing soldiers contradict each other. Earlier, when a shell struck the town in bright daylight, everyone went undercover in a flash. In the shortest of time, the town was completely cleared of the small troop squads with all their vehicles pulled out of all alleys. Suddenly there was fuel and the repairs did not seem to have been so necessary.

We are completely on our own now. No more military. The sudden emptiness and silence actually feels weird. From now on we have an effective way to get rid of the military vehicles parked at any of the houses. All we have to say is that the town is under fire, and they roll out. The air attack of the Jabos has not yet waned. A few days ago, when the First Aid stations were still in town, the kitchen wagon of one of these sanitary units was housed in the rectory yard. One of these

Jabos attacked the kitchen wagon with an on-board weapon. During the attack a projectile pierced the window of my bedroom, tore off the window latch, shattered the lamp fixture, broke through the door of the wardrobe, and landed in a cardboard box at the bottom of the wardrobe. Luckily nobody was in the room at the time. For the last few days, I mostly sleep in the cellar. During these artillery attacks, with constant shelling, night after night, sleep only comes if you are deep under cover. This morning, when it was still dark, we were awakened by dull clatter from the street. It was like heavy vehicles were rolling over stones. Are the tanks rolling forward towards the front again? When I went to church for the early Sunday mass, I saw a vehicle with a massive cannon being pulled up the mountain by 24 horses. When I asked where they were heading I was told to the next village - about 2 miles away. I think it was a 24 dm Cannon. Well, the people there will be happy about these guests! Throughout early mass, the noise continued in the street. When it got light, they unrigged the horses and left the canon. They left this stupid thing right in front of the rectory. Without any camouflage. To make matters worse, we had a really bright day. It's cannon fodder for the Jabos. Even the cellar was not safe enough for me that morning. Like many of the other residents - there were still several more of these cannons in the town - we also pack necessities and head towards the school cellar, which is just outside the town.

But the schoolyard is also full of military vehicles. That means we'd go from the frying pan into the fire. In addition, the first artillery volley hit near the school just after our arrival. So back to the town again. Let's surrender to our destiny, but contrary to everyone's expectations, the rest of the day is quiet, without any more significant events. After dark, we are slowly but surely relieved of our unwelcome guests and their horrible cannons.

February 13, 1945

The whole area is now under constant artillery fire at night. During the daytime the streets throughout the parish communities are only navigable at risk of death. From time to time we hear shells here and there. I only hope I don't have to make any out-of-town house calls now. This morning I had another funeral. I held the memorial at the cemetery in the dusk. The cemetery is constantly under fire, so I did the internment the evening before. I had blessed the deceased by myself. Having relatives present is no longer possible. When I return to the tomb this morning, I find a deep shell crater, remnants of the nightly shelling, right in front of the grave. When I come home from the funeral, a man is waiting for me from a branch parish about 3 miles away. I have to make a house-call to administer last rights. After a quick breakfast I set off. I try to go the normal, shorter way, but an artillery volley falls just before I get to my destination and forces me to turn back. I make it through on a more guarded detour. After I administer the last rights, I give Holy Communion to two other sick people in the village. I walk home in the evening. Just as I reach the town limits the shooting begins again. I only hope that I don't have to leave town again until all this is over.

February 18, 1945

All indications are that our unsustainable situation is slowly coming to an end. Today, only the locals come to the Sunday service. I had asked soldiers to let the people of the surrounding villages know, that for now they should not come to town. To let those people come to church now means to send them to certain death. We all yearn for the offensive that will hopefully start soon from the other side. Because the current state of affairs is impossible. We have long given up hope that we will get through this unscathed. What does it look like in the town? There are hardly any windows left. Instead of glass, windows are covered with wood or cardboard. In the bomb craters, which gape next to the main supply road leading through the town, lie horse carcasses, vehicle parts, and scraps of uniforms. The homes near the bomb sites look bad, for the most part uninhabited and uninhabitable. We sink up to our ankles in mud in the streets. Images from my military time in the First World War rise before my mind's eye. That it had to come to this! The war could have ended last summer. It was already lost then. Now our beautiful hometown is becoming a debris field. Today, the local government has left, together with most officials and leading National Socialists. They plan to go to the Mosel river and then on across the Rhine. We have been left to our fate, but for that we are thankful. It is a relief to be freed from this scourge. Only a few officials defied the strict evacuation orders of the Party leadership. Most officials are gone. I wonder if they will regret it soon! Of course it is anything but pleasant here. Others, mostly newcomers, have left the town one after the other during the last few weeks. Thus, the number of townspeople gets smaller, but the prospect is getting better that our remaining food supplies will last.

Resupply is no longer possible. Slowly but surely the cellar has become our permanent residence. All of our food has been brought here. For the days when we are not likely to cook in the kitchen, canned food will have to do. Clothes and bedding is packed. Everything that can be stored in the cellar, and is not already there, is taken downstairs. We all suspect, in the next few days it will get even more serious.

February 19, 1945

What a restless night! Once again I tried to sleep in a real bed upstairs, but the constant hissing of the shells and the subsequent explosions kept me up all night. Weeks ago I had felt fairly safe in my upstairs "bunker." That's what we called the bedroom, whose window we had walled up at the end of summer. I will probably need to sleep in the cellar from now on.

The impacts had to be very close. Even after sunrise, it does not stop. By 7:00AM it had always been quiet, so that I could hold my service. Most days it remained calm at least during the morning. We've gotten used to this routine and are thankful to the Americans for being so considerate with their shooting. Today, however, they seem to have changed their tactics. Judging by the impacts, the shells are all landing in the same place in the southwestern part of town. There is a bridge over the Prüm river in what we call "little Venice." Where they shooting at the bridge? The shells come at intervals of exactly half an hour. If the Americans stick to this order, we could do our job during the breaks. I get dressed and watch. After exactly half an hour, the next shell falls. I use the interim until the next one to reach the hospital, where I hold the Holy Mass in the chapel. From the people at the hospital I now also learn where the shells are hitting. It is, as I suspected. Slightly below the above-mentioned bridge, the river bends 90° to the south at a rock cliff, which rises vertically about 150 feet. This is the target of the impacts. The two perpendicular rock faces form an ideal splinter catch, so that there is no danger for the town, as long as the Americans don't change trajectory. Only the mill located on one side of the river, below the bridge, is getting hit with shrapnel. When I return home after the service, another shell comes down. Exactly to the minute it comes. I'm able to watch the impact from the higher street level where I stand. In the town everything proceeds its usual course. We are already front-hardened. The shooting lasts until about noon. The shells come on the dot, punctually, every half hour. As soon as one is "due" we go into the cellar as a precaution. When the impact is over, everyone goes about their usual work. From today on, I will only sleep in the cellar.

February 20, 1945

Towards evening the artillery fire comes again. When I pass by the church the next morning, the meadow on the other side of the Prüm is covered with shell craters. The pavement on this side of the church is littered with broken slate, stones and mortar. Only now do I realize that the church was hit. The roof on the river-side is perforated. The vaulted ceiling is still intact, only a few holes can be seen from the inside, but the floor in that part of the church is covered with wood splinters and rubble. There is a lot of dust on the pews. After Mass, which I celebrate in peace in the hospital chapel, I sweep the passage in front of my confessional, so that the people don't drag the rubble throughout the whole church during the next service. I have to do the work myself, since the cleaning lady no longer ventures out of her house, or better, out of her cellar. During the day, I also learn the reason for the massive shooting in just this spot. Yesterday evening a German military communications group was parked next to the only house that is standing there. Again and again we make the observation that the German Wehrmacht has no consideration for the civilian population anymore. One has the impression that some even feel a certain malicious joy when the bombs and shells turn our houses into rubble. Many of the soldiers are bombed out at home. One of them once said to me: "I myself have nothing left, so you need nothing more!"

February 21, 1945

Last night the shells struck the town nonstop. Some hits were so close that the cellar was shaking. One of the shells must have hit next to the rectory, if not in the rectory itself.

The next morning reveals a gruesome picture of devastation. The rectory had been spared, at least as far as I can see. I do not dare to go into the garden as the shells are still falling at irregular intervals. But the neighbor's property has gotten hit. The roof of the utility building, which closes the courtyard to the rear, was half torn away. There must have been several impacts. I use a small break from the fire to rush to the hospital. I hope that it is safer on this side of town and that at least I could celebrate a mass, since the impacts in my estimation are mainly in the town center. As I hurry past the church, I can see that the sacristy facing the street was destroyed. The courtyard amid the high linden trees on the south side of the church looks devastated. Some trees are destroyed by shells and lay in a tumbled mess. I see several shell craters in the street. My heart sinks, but I keep on walking to the hospital. Apart from the hospital staff and patients, only about half a dozen people from the town have come to the mass in the chapel. The others do not dare to go out on the street because of the ongoing shellfire. Around the hospital, too, one can see the traces of the nightly bombardment. Streets and houses have received hits. There is no safety even here on the outskirts of town. Nevertheless, I start the church service. During prayer we hear the 1st explosion. I stop for a moment and listen: a hit in the middle of the town. I continue prayers in the hope that I can finish the mass. After completion of the prayer, the 2nd explosion; This time very close. I have to give up so as not to expose the congregation to danger. I give the instruction to go to the cellar at once, hurry to take off my robes and lay them on the Altar, and then hurry to the cellar. Until further notice, I cancel all services. I wait for the next explosion, then head towards my own cellar. Now we will probably not be able to leave the cellar even during the day. Hopefully everything will pass quickly! On the way to the rectory I have to stop at three other cellars to seek protection from the shells. From one of the cellars I have to watch as another explosion hit the church. What will remain of our stately church! My relatives are anxiously waiting for me at the rectory. All the other neighbors are already in the cellar of the neighboring house Schmillen, where we have sought shelter during the days for the last few weeks. This reasonably spacious, heated basement will probably be our home for the days to come. We are here with five families, a total of 23 people, men, women and children. For the first time we are staying here overnight. Since there is no room to set up a cot, I spend the night on a hard

wooden chair. The shooting continues without interruption. At irregular intervals, which can no longer be calculated, the shells burst in all different parts of the town. The war with its horrors hovers over the houses and streets.

February 22, 1945

I didn't sleep much last night. Sitting on the hard chair was not pleasant, but what a blessing that we didn't spend the night in our basement. A shell hit right near the root cellar door. The large crater and, even more than that, the damage suggests a pretty heavy caliber. The outer of the two cellar doors, studded with zinc sheeting, is completely fragmented; one door was thrown about 30 feet. The inner door shows gaping cracks. A thick beam, which was used as a bar across the door, is broken like a match. The two parts were thrown across the cots in our cellar, it could have cost several lives. During a break in the firing, I manage to block off the outside entrance to the cellar with the inner door, which had been torn off its hinges. We still have all of our valuables stored in the cellar. Then I run back to safety quickly before the next shells hit.

Our corner of the town seems to be the main target, even though the whole town is embattled by the impacts. Just in front of the rectory, a rear access road (or rather access path) meets the road that runs through the town right to the war front. I never would have guessed that would matter much. Until 1:00PM the shells continue crashing down irregularly. Sometimes there are two, often three hits in a row. We use the short break after such explosions to cross the street from our neighbors to the rectory. We hadn't yet gotten everything we need for a long-term stay. Some things you don't miss until you need them. When we entered the neighbor's cellar yesterday morning, we did not expect this would be a permanent arrangement. The emergency apartment next to the rectory is the most endangered. Therefor we bring out my tenant's wood burning stove into our neighbor's basement; at least it's safe there, and at the same time we will have cooking facilities. If the shooting goes on, you can no longer cook in the rooms above ground. At 1:00PM the last explosion happens. It is quiet for a couple of hours. We breathe. Immediately there is some life on the street. Some hurry to the baker. Others quickly run into their homes to collect more supplies. Everyone has now settled in their cellars. Often several neighboring families together. It turns 3:00PM, then 4:00PM, and still it's quiet. We can hear children in the street again. For a short time, it is as if the war had been forgotten. I use the peace in the cellar to pray. My mother and sister have gone outside. The children are chopping wood outside in front of the tunnel-like vaulted cellar entrance. Then suddenly, quite unexpectedly at 5:00PM an explosion. It's an impact in the immediate vicinity. Everyone panics and rushes back into the cellar from above and from outside. We already hear screaming and shouting from outside. My sister is not here yet. I see my mother excitedly gesticulating in front of the basement.

It becomes a terrible certainty that one of us has been hit. Then some of our cellar roommates, including my sister, bring in a woman with a bloody face. It is Mrs. K., my tenant. She was in the yard across the street when the shell struck nearby. She could still see the firelight flashing, as she already felt a blow on the head and the warm blood stream down over her face. A doctor is not available, especially now that the bombardment has started again. Fortunately, we have a trained nurse among us. Quickly we examine the quivering and agitated crying woman and her bleeding head wound. She is the mother of four children. Thank God, the wound is not bad. The splinter does not seem to be in there anymore. We wash out the wound and bind it. Because the cellar serves as an air raid shelter, we are well equipped with medical gear. Who knows what else we need! This first wounded person in our cellar community makes us all a little more cautious. To get a little sleep for the coming nights, I bring down a padded armchair from the apartment above. Now the second night of permanent residence can begin in our community cellar.

February 23, 1945

My first concern after getting up this morning was for the rectory across the street. Whether it still stands after the hellish bombardment of this night? As soon as a short break in shelling makes it possible, we scurry across at once. Since none of the doors can be closed anymore, a short walk through the house suffices to see if everything is still there. We don't know if the Wehrmacht is still in town. Everyone has moved back into defensive positions. Occasionally at night we hear troops pull through, probably reinforcements for the front. We soon realize that there was a visitor in the rectory last night. There are several things missing. Even in the basement things are gone, including women's clothing and my shoes. Certain evidence raises the suspicion that it may have been civilians.

At first, I don't want to believe that. I don't want to believe that a civilian has the courage to steal during such murderous shelling, especially since our corner has been hit hard again. In two spots our garden wall is cracked, in front of it are two big shell craters. As a precaution, between the individual impacts, we bring our most valuables over into our current cellar.

In the afternoon during a break in shellfire I run over to the church. I have to recover the Blessed Sacrament, because you don't know what will happen to the church. What a sight it is there. And even more inside. The outer sacristy wall has collapsed. Inside, the cabinets are shattered and torn apart with their contents now a tangled mess of wood splinters, stones, debris and dust. With difficulty, I make my way over the debris heap to the interior of the church. Here, too, debris and destruction. In front of the communion rail lies a pile of stones and rubble. The vaulted ceiling is smashed in, an area of at least 10 square feet. The ceiling beams are shredded. One or more shells must have penetrated the roof. Above me I see blue sky. The choir stalls have remained intact. Last fall I had already brought the valuable altar figures to safety. They are from 1771, the construction period of the church. Quickly I open the tabernacle and empty the monstrance. I bring out the ciborium with the tabernacle, hide it under my coat and hurry back to the cellar. In an unoccupied part of the cellar I hide the chalice with the precious holy content. In the evening of this day, as is usual lately, Wehrmacht soldiers come to visit us in the cellar. They want to have something to drink. I ask them about the situation? We would like to know more about the state of the front. One of them told us that they belong to the demolition squad and have orders to blow up all bridges and roads, after all German soldiers have crossed the Prüm river.

"When will that be, I ask."

"The exact time is communicated to us by courier." He answered. "It may still be tonight, so then the front is not far away."

He says, "The last units of the German Wehrmacht are approaching the town now."

An indescribable feeling comes over us with this announcement. Then our time of suffering will soon be over. I try to make it clear to the man that his detonation campaign cannot stop the advance of the Americans, so why even destroy the bridges that are so urgently needed by civilians. I think of the railway bridge just before the town, whose destruction will paralyze rail traffic for years to come. The soldier also sees this, but says: "Orders are orders!"

February 24, 1945

We get no sleep that night, because the shells howl and crash, with about five hundred hits, someone counted. And suddenly, in the morning, a muffled detonation amid the crash of the shells. Then a noise as if it was raining stones. This repeated 5 or 6 times. Detonations! Now we are the war front. There is no more German Wehrmacht between us and the Americans. Because of the detonation of the bridges we are cut off from the part of the town that's on the east-side of the river.

Yesterday, I was called to visit the neighboring cellar on the other side of the street. The shell, which had wounded Mrs. K.'s head, had also injured a boy's forearm. The doctor had not come yet, although he had been called several times, and I went over early this morning. I brought communion for everyone in the cellar. I found the boy had a fever of 104° and the wound looked bad. After a short preparatory speech, I gave the general absolution to all. All received communion solemnly. The continuous shooting kept me there for three hours - until about 11:00AM and then I dared to run back across the street.

As a result of the explosions, the road has been torn open at various spots. This has ruptured the main water pipe. Now all the cellar communities have to get their water from the Weiherbach stream flowing in back of the town. Because of the continuous bombardment this is a dangerous thing! Now people are always rushing past our cellar during every major mortar break. In the afternoon finally we learn from those with a view of the other side of the Prüm river, that which we have all been eager to hear. The first Amis (Americans) were sighted around noon. Their troops are across the river. Larger formations have been spotted in the forested areas on the mountain beyond, as well as between the houses up on the hill. When will they come across? At any rate, we hear the news with a sense of relief.

February 25, 1945 Sunday.

The fifth day of our permanent stay in the neighbor's cellar. I have brought everything necessary together, to at least today on Sunday celebrate a Mass. We notified the neighboring cellars. Whoever can come should be in our cellar by 10:00AM. The day before, our female housemates had wet-mopped the entire cellar floor. The cots were neatly made, whatever we could do to make it presentable we did in order to have a sacred service. A small table - the space was very limited - served as an altar. It was a real catacomb worship service. Outside, the noise of war was howling, and here in the subterranean cellar community, the King of Peace was soon to make His entrance. Everyone was deeply moved. I give a short talk to prepare us for General Absolution. All who were at the holy mass took holy communion. This holy Celebration was probably the highlight of our cellar stay.

The most urgent prayer going up to Heaven, from the bottom of everyone's heart, may have been the prayer for a quick ending of our daily affliction. The rest of the day went by in the usual way. Gradually, a certain pattern had emerged. We usually got up around 8:00AM and had breakfast. Everybody would sit on their own cot with their plates on their knees. Lunch and dinner were cooked together for everyone. Everyone gave what they had. The family groups alternated cooking lunch and dinner, and doing the dishes. Of the children, the boys first had to get the carbide lamps prepared in the morning, then they cut wood. The women usually did sowing and needlepoint in the afternoons. We still had retreating soldiers come into the cellar occasionally. We would quickly write a little mail, which was then transported as field post with the soldier as the sender. It was the only way to let our distant relatives know what was happening with us. For lighting during the day we used remnants of wax in small, homemade lamps. Despite all the shelling, the two bakers of the town continued baking bread. The bread was then distributed during breaks in the firing. So long as the flour supply was sufficient, there was no danger that we needed to starve. Once, from our cellar, we were able to observe how American artillery silenced a German firing division. The German position was on a hill above the town; one we could see well from our cellar. For several days we heard the sound of their guns. It sounded like a very loud, bright drum roll. One morning, about 10:00AM, some smoke shells came from over there with dull sounding impacts. A few more minutes and then the shooting erupted like a hurricane. This lasted several minutes and we heard loud crashing and howling, and then we saw dust and fiery flamethrowers. Then suddenly silence. We waited tensely until the dust and smoke settled and the view cleared. We still could see a few soldiers rushing down, hunched and bent, two men carried a seemingly seriously injured or even dead soldier over the hill. Then silence – later I will go visit that spot and see if any casualties are buried there.

February 26, 1945

At dawn this morning I make my way to the hospital. It's the first time I've walked through the town since last Wednesday. The Mother Superior urges me to bring the Blessed Sacrament from the hospital into safety. How the town has changed in the last few days! Hardly any windows are intact. At almost every house the window frames are gaping open wide. The doors are torn off. Everything is open. The walls, as far as they are not penetrated, are bespattered with shrapnel holes. On the roads, which are torn open in places, there are mountains of slate shingles, stones, splinters of wood; here and there car wrecks. At the main thoroughfare it looks even bleaker. Horse carcasses lay almost every few steps. Remains of vehicles and mud. The streets are completely empty. The town looks abandoned. Every now and then I see smoke rising from the cellar hatches, the only sign that shows the presence of life. I hurry as fast as I can, shielded by houses. Across the river – only 40 to 50 feet away – is the American Army. As soon as I'll get to the higher part of the road, which is visible to the enemy, I'll need to run as fast as I can. Before that, I take a break in a cellar. There's already a shell hissing over me. It flies beyond the town to the retreating Wehrmacht troops. When I reach my destination, I find out that a German artillery observer has occupied the hospital. I can hear his loud phone calls to the retreating army. On the ground floor there is still a troop of soldiers who have taken up position in the hospital. The sisters and patients stay in the cellar. I give the general absolution to all and then offer them Holy Communion. I hide the Blessed Sacrament under my coat and move through town again, from cellar to cellar to get home. Along the way, everyone is astonished, and they are so happy to see me. Everyone has so many questions, but I can't stay long, because I have to go on and besides, I carry the tabernacle with me. Everyone, without exception, receives the general absolution and holy communion. These are unforgettable moments for everyone.

February 27, 1945

The impacts are now behind us on the hills. The two fronts are so close to each other, separated only by the 10 to 12-foot-wide river and some shore areas. In a way that's an advantage now. For neither the American nor the German artillery are firing so accurately that they could still target the opposing front, without endangering their own. The Americans now shoot over us onto the ascending hills behind the town, but that does not concern us anymore. We even stand outside temporarily and watch an American airplane, which majestically draws circles at a very slow pace, like a giant bird. Ever since I had to constantly sleep in a seated position in a chair, I've had such a desire to be able to stretch out properly again. Around 1 PM, I just settle down on one of the cots, suddenly a murderous shooting begins. It's a machine-gun, which sounds like it's right in front of the cellar, and artillery volleys crashing in between. In the midst of this noise a second machine gun rattles, and soon after a third. At first I think one of the German machine-gun nests built into the riverbank is shooting for all it's worth, but I soon become certain that something more is happening. There has to be real street fighting going on. The women start to pray the rosary. I heave myself from my bed, dress completely, and already one of our cellar dwellers comes rushing in with the message: "There's a tank in front of the house!"

"German or American?" I ask. "I do not know."

That the Germans still would pull tanks so far forward is unthinkable. Could the Americans be here? That would be an end to all our fears. It's hard to imagine! I had to have certainty. I cautiously crawl toward the street on hands and feet. There it is. A tank. Its gun barrel is threateningly pointed at the house, and in front of the tank paces a soldier with his rifle ready to fire, peering in all directions. I immediately recognized the foreign uniforms: the Americans! I hurried back into the cellar: "They are here!" Thank God! A million thoughts tumble through our minds. One outweighs the other. Now the war with all its horrors, is over for us; the Third Reich is done here now! We got ready for the first meeting with our previous enemies. In front of the cellar we put out a white flag; a quickly made inscription proclaims in English that the cellar only contained civilians. For quite some time we wait in suspense until heavy footsteps herald the approach of the first soldier. Briefly he looks from the outside into the cellar. "Are there any soldiers here?" he questions, which we could honestly deny, then he disappears again. Meanwhile, the shooting moves on to the middle of the town. Tank sounds are audible from there. After about an hour we hear more steps. This time from several people. Two wounded American soldiers are brought to us, one injured in the foot, the other in the head. Blood had already soaked through their fresh bandages. They seem to be in severe pain. We make beds for them on chairs, and as they demand drink we offered them cold coffee leftover from breakfast. They gratefully accept. In return, they hand out cigarettes. From the guard standing in front of the cellar entrance, we are told that until further notice no one is allowed to leave the cellar. With pleasure we accept this temporary restriction of our freedom.

We now have the happy certainty that the Nazi rule is over and life in dignity and freedom can begin. Towards evening, the space of the cellar, where the wounded had first been laid, is filled with American soldiers. The wounded themselves were taken away at dawn by ambulances. Above us in the rooms of the apartment, restless heavy footsteps echo and rattle constantly. Troops are billeting for the night. We ourselves are still not allowed to leave the cellar. We would have loved to know how this first day of fighting had gone in this part of town. We receive only shrugs when we ask the American soldiers. Several explosions sound in the evening and during the night, but they sound like they are already at a distance. They are probably German shells. In one of the rooms above us about two dozen German prisoners are brought in towards evening: the catch of the day. Whatever else is left of the German troops in the village would probably have gone underground when the enemy approached. The prisoners of war seemed happy that the war is over for them as well. We are not allowed to speak with them.

February 28, 1945

Throughout the morning, columns move incessantly through the village. Around lunchtime our "guests" move out. The advance seems to go on and we are allowed to leave the cellar. My first visit is to the rectory. Now we no longer need to be prepared for shells every minute. We cross the street through ankle deep mud and have a look at what the war has left us. Only now do we see the full extent of the destruction. Three or four panes of glass are all that are still intact of our many windows. The interior doors are completely torn away, and in large areas the plaster has fallen down from the ceiling and walls. The high courtyard wall of the rectory is mostly rubble. Several shells must have smashed them. The ceilings have collapsed in the rooms facing this direction, the furniture is partly smashed. And everywhere dirt, debris and dust. The only room in the house that is reasonably habitable is the kitchen, only without doors and windows. It takes a while to get the whole picture of the devastation. Rubble and debris, partly from the house, partly from the outbuilding, which stands without a roof, covered the yard many feet high. Broken rafters stick up in the air. Again, the traces of several shell hits. We can't even enter the garden. Uprooted trees and branches cover vegetable beds and paths. On the way back to our cellar home, where we are still living for the time being, I consider not moving back into the rectory. I don't think it's possible to make this ruin habitable once more. Today we don't eat lunch in the cellar anymore. Being able to sit properly at a laid table is a symbol of slowly resuming normalcy. Out in the streets, motorized American columns are constantly pulling through. We are shocked at the sight of an army equipped most practically and with an overwhelming abundance of the most modern war material. And against that Hitler dared his war! "Poor Germany!" We spend the rest of the day covering the windows of the rectory.

March 1, 1945

On the orders of the American commander, this afternoon a representative from each family is ordered to the church square to receive the first orders of the military occupation government. As we gather, there's such joy. We have not seen each other for days. From all the cellars they come. Dusty, their faces pale and gray, and reflecting the horror and the worries of the last few days. Everyone has questions and stories to tell.

Thank God! Nobody died in the last few days. There may have been a few wounded. In the part of town beyond the river that had been occupied by the Americans days ago, German shells seriously wounded some civilians. They were brought out by the occupying forces and sent to their military hospital. We think that is in Luxembourg. The enemy's concern for these victims of warfare was exemplary. The commander appeared with his interpreter. The first regulations proclaim the dissolution and prohibition of the NSDAP and all divisions; the abolition of all Nazi laws! So the thousand-year Reich is over. So ends the unbearable terror, the mental torture, the insults and so much subhuman behavior. It's Over! But at what price? Sunk in a stream of blood and tears and destruction. All the inhabitants take in this proclamation in admirable calm. Then, however, there is another declaration what limits our newly gained freedom: until further notice, we must stay in our homes. Nobody is allowed to enter the street. It is, as the interpreter informs me, for the protection of the population, since we are still on the war front. In two days, he hoped, a limited permit would be granted. How necessary this regulation was, we would learn quickly. For we had not broken up yet, when shells struck nearby. Our euphoria was also dampened by the fact that all homes occupied by Americans had to be cleared of German civilians immediately.

March 2, 1945

The first Friday of the month. I celebrate Holy Mass for the first time since Sunday. But not in the cellar anymore. This time we set up a room in the home of our hosts. The entire cellar community is gathered, as well as some neighbors who sneak in despite the curfew.

We have every reason to give thanks for the rescue out of many dangers. Everything could have been much worse. After all, we have kept our hometown, and we have kept enough living space and household goods to be able to rebuild this life.

March 3, 1945

Shooting is becoming rarer. Here and there a detonation suddenly startles us. You can tell, the war is moving away from our area. Of course, the roads are still hard to conquer. Unstoppable, like a chain that never tears, vehicle after vehicle, tank after tank rolls past us. The American Reserves seem inexhaustible. We are becoming more and more aware of how frivolously our so-called leaders ushered us into this disaster and how terrible it is, if one underestimates their enemy. At about 3:00PM the commander let me know that tomorrow, Sunday at 10 AM I would be able to hold the first public service in the church. From then on until 5:00PM the curfew is suspended. We are overjoyed to hear this! Immediately I look for a couple of boys, girls and women, to quickly prepare the church for the service. For the first time since the day I salvaged the Blessed Sacrament, I enter the church again. All the doors hang tattered in their hinges. Otherwise no new damage had occurred. In the short time available, it's impossible to clean the whole church of dust and debris, so at least we clean the altar area. We clear the rubble out with wheelbarrows. Then we dust the altar and finally mop the floor. The choir area has the least amount of damage. We find some shrapnel in the altar cloth and the old-fashioned choir stalls. This had torn small holes, but that's only noticeable up close. Otherwise everything is here, even the vaulted ceiling remains mainly intact. The sacristy is unusable; so we set up a table under the organ loft to lay out the garments and items needed for worship.

March 4, 1945 Sunday.

We eagerly approach the end of our curfew, which is also set for the beginning of the church service. For the first time during these anxious days, the community is back together to celebrate the holy sacraments. Our branch churches are not yet allowed to come because, beyond the local boundaries, there is still no permission to travel. Also, some locals had moved out to neighboring villages in the last few weeks. That means the church is only half full. Nevertheless, the singing of those who attend the service fills the majestic, now oh-so-badly shabby interior of the venerable house of God. Everywhere there is still rubble from the bombardments. It's cold, the wet wind blows through the open window frames. Luckily it doesn't rain, so we are not particularly bothered by the torn and broken parts of the ceiling and roof. But all these impressions are outweighed by the consideration that we can now celebrate our services, for the first time in many weeks, quietly, undisturbed by rattled nerves and the fear of shells. In the brief address of this evocative service, I confidently share with those present the feeling of deep gratitude that we, in the first place, owe to God for salvation from the perils of these last weeks. In the remarkable protection which, despite all occurrences, our hometown has nevertheless found, we may also know the fruit of the special veneration that the Mother of God enjoys with us. We never want to forget that, and as soon as time permits, we express this conviction through a special act. Then in the near future we will need two things above all else: courage and true Christian charity, to face the terrible destruction and discouraging rubble that the war has left us and to face the terrible misery that is a consequence of years of madness. The way to the communion rail can only to be reached across rubble heaps. Now that we have permission to go outside for at least a few hours during the day, cleaning and makeshift repair of our church should be the first thing we tackle. The organ is sound and playable despite the shelling that took place over the town and the church. In this way, she too was able to let her voice ring in this service, which was sure to be unforgettable for all participants. With a heartfelt

"Deo gratias" (Thanks be to God) - the measured ending of the Mass, we concluded this first public church service after the second great world war ended here for us.

Thus the writer of these lines also concludes his memoir..

Appendix

Note from translator:

Waxweiler after the War *by Uta (Irsch) Milewski*

This part of the appendix started out as a one-page note to describe Waxweiler after the war and to connect my family's history to the town. As I began to write, memories came flooding in. If you're not interested, skip the adventure and fast forward to the pictures at the end of the book.

I was born 11 years after the war ended. Throughout my early life in the town of Waxweiler, the war was a daily topic of conversation in my family. Every adult had experienced it either as a soldier with the Wehrmacht or as a civilian when the front moved through. Pastor Kiefer's journal reflects how my family talked not only about the war, but also about Hitler and the American occupation after the war.

There was somewhat of a love/hate relationship towards the Ami. This is what Germans called Americans. The word was used in the singular as if all of them were just one person. The Ami was a former enemy who had delivered Germans from Hitler but then also controlled them. The Ami occupied the southwest part of Germany. Britain, Russia and France occupied the rest. Occupation ended in 1949, but the Ami continued to maintain military bases. Two of them were near Waxweiler: Bitburg and Spangdahlem. They were Air Force bases, and fighter jet flyovers became the daily norm in Waxweiler.

I lived with my family in this small town of a thousand people in walking distance to the church, the school, the grocery store, our grandparents, great-aunts, aunts, uncles and cousins.

In the 50's life was self-contained in the town and surrounding villages. People worked close to where they lived. Almost everything we needed was available nearby.

I recall that only a few houses were still damaged during my youth. Two prominent houses in the town had no mortar on the outside but were completely intact inside. The former District Court was leveled and we could only see the arches of the cellar windows peeking out of the ground. Everything else had been repaired within a short time after the war.

When my father, Josef Irsch, was first drafted into the Wehrmacht, he was stationed in a bunker at the Westwall.

My father was later deployed to Norway and then to Russia. I remember pictures of him in a white winter uniform on skis.

My father had wanted golden wedding rings, but there were none in Germany in 1941. So he drove to Belgium with a friend, where the two persuaded two Belgian girls to pretend to be engaged to them, so they could buy gold rings. What the two girls got as a reward is beyond my knowledge, but the whole matter is said to have taken three days.

My parents were married on August 2, 1941 in Prüm, my mother's home town. My father got a few days leave and then had to head back into combat.

Back in Russia, during a battle, a pointy grenade pinned his foot to the ground and he couldn't pull it out. A buddy yanked it out and threw it just before it exploded.

September 15, 1942 was a sunny autumn day in Russia. In the distance my father saw the golden towers of the Moscow Kremlin through his binoculars. My brother, Rudolf, told me the date and I wondered why he knew it so exactly. It was the day he was born and after my father returned from Russia my parents connected the dots.

In Russia again in 1944 my father was a sergeant-in-chief and platoon leader of an anti-tank battery with three cannons of relatively small caliber, which were rarely effective against the Russian tanks and were therefore called tank knockers by the soldiers. Things did not look good for the German army and they began a retreat.

On the retreat, which had been reasonably orderly until then, the soldiers had not had any food for three days and had hardly had any ammunition left. My father's unit stayed in a small house, the residents of which allegedly had no food.

Sleeping hungry and waking up hungry, my father wanted to put on the wedding ring he had taken off in the evening. The ring fell to the ground and disappeared into a crack. My father didn't want to pull out without his ring, so he and his soldiers looked for a basement door or a trap door because there was obviously a room underneath.

Behind the house, they found a staircase leading down below and a door under some brushwood. The ring and a pile of potatoes lay in the basement. My father ordered his soldiers to stow half of the potatoes in the front compartment of the cannon where normally the ammunition was stored. While the soldiers were loading up potatoes, the guard yelled: "Herr Sergeant, we have to get out of here, Russian tanks are coming in." However, my father did not want to leave the potatoes and ordered a shot on the tanks so that they did not approach too quickly. They of course fired back, the neighboring units noticed that, there was a skirmish in which the German troops advanced 20 km. Of course, everything was documented at the time, and the commander asked my father why he shot. He wisely avoided mentioning the ring and the potatoes and said that the Russians suddenly showed up and that he had to defend himself. The commander, as a higher rank, got the IRON CROSS FIRST CLASS and my father, who was actually the hero of the story, got the IRON CROSS SECOND CLASS.

Nazi propaganda at the time showed newsreels with soldiers crying out to Hitler with their last breath. My father said that in reality they cried out to their mothers.

By the spring of 1945 my father was with the Infantry on the French border. In early April, things looked badly for the Germans. My father's troop was ready to surrender. They raised the white flag, but the Americans had been fooled too many times and continued shooting. My father was hit. The bone in his right arm was severed above the elbow by a shell from a tank. He was declared dead and put in a morgue. When he came to, his arm was amputated in the Lazaret (military hospital) in Heidelberg. This happened a month before the war officially ended in May 1945.

My grandparents Matthias and Maria Irsch, lived in a small house near the hospital in Waxweiler. My father and his eight siblings were born and raised in that small house. My grandparents spent all the war years there. They lost their son, Alois, in Russia. Another son, Robert, spent years in a Russian POW camp, and their son, Josef, my father, lost his right arm and his livelihood as a master tailor. Once, when a cousin, a local Nazi visited his home, my grandfather spoke openly against Hitler. The Nazi threatened to report him, but Matthias Irsch said, "I will speak the truth in my own home."

My father, too, had not been fooled by Hitler's bombastic speeches. He often spoke of his desire to shoot Hitler when he was at the Waxweiler train station in August of 1938. That would have been death to our entire family. So would have been his refusal to fight in the war. Deserters and their families were hung, without trial, on the nearest trees. He often considered how much suffering could have been avoided, and how many millions of lives could have been saved if he had done it.

My father had been threatened and beaten up several times by Nazis for attending Catholic Youth Group and for working for Jewish tailors. He helped one of the Jewish tailors sew all of his paper money into the lining of his winter coat, so the man could take his wealth with him when he escaped to Argentina.

My maternal grandmother, Anna Hermes, a widow, lived twelve miles North of Waxweiler, in the city of Prüm. While my father was deployed, my mother, Maria (Hermes) Irsch lived with her mother and two sisters, Gertrud and Sophie, in Prüm. My aunt Sophie had a birth defect. She had been a difficult breach birth and as a result had a limp and some learning delays. Under Hitler, the retarded were not allowed to reproduce and Sophie was sterilized as a young woman.

The family from Prüm were evacuated on September 14, 1944, two days after my sister Irmburg's birth, when my brother Rudolf was 2 years old. They were loaded onto a Red Cross truck. Another young mother was unable to nurse her two-day old baby on that trip, so my mother nursed both babies.

They were taken first to the city of Solingen and later to the tiny village of Wehrden on the Weser, where they stayed with my grandmother's relatives until the end of the war.

I had always wondered why Prüm was evacuated and Waxweiler wasn't. I found the answer in this journal.

Our extended family all attended the Catholic Church in Waxweiler every Sunday. I imagine my grandparents were at every church service mentioned in this journal. So were all our other relatives who lived in Waxweiler at that time.

As of this writing my aunt Josefine (Fini) Irsch born in 1927 is my father's only living sibling. She continues to tell much more of the family history than I remember. My brother promised to write it all down.

Fini was a teen-ager throughout the war years and so was her future husband, Josef Schwickerath. Josef's mother told me and my cousins many war stories while we gathered around the Schwickerath's kitchen table watching her peel apples or potatoes. She was such a good story teller, I foolishly often wished I could have experienced the war myself. Some of the details in this journal I recalled from her stories, especially about the days in the earth bunkers.

After the war, statistics were released which showed that 20% of Waxweiler was destroyed. The nearby town of Lünebach was 82% destroyed.

The most poignant moment described by Pastor Kiefer was the church service when 1,000 male voices sang a hymn. I found the Translation of that hymn by J.M. Haydn: "Hier liegt vor deiner Majestät"

> *On bended knee a guilty race,*
> *Before Thee we appear;*
> *O grant us Lord, thy saving grace,*
> *Our sighs of sorrow hear.*
> *That we're unworthy, Lord, we own,*
> *But let Thy mercy still be shown,*
> *And on us sinners pity take,*
> *For thine and our sweet Jesus' sake*

The Apostle Peter once said, *"Repent therefore and be converted, that your sins may be blotted out, so that times of refreshing may come from the presence of the Lord..."* (Acts 3:19). I believe that is what happened in Waxweiler. The humility declared aloud in this hymn changed the atmosphere, because: *"God resists the proud, but gives grace to the humble"* (1 Peter 5:5).

For those who wonder that after all that bombing and shelling only 20% of the town was destroyed I want to explain that many of the bombs fell on the mountains around Waxweiler. We often found bomb craters while playing in the woods.

Another factor is the construction method used on the older houses in town. From 1960 to 1974 our family lived in an apartment above my mother's clothing store, Bekleidungshaus Irsch, which was located, in the oldest part of town, kiddy corner across from the church. The outside walls of the building where at least 2 feet thick, built from fieldstones and mortar. The inner walls were cinder block, covered in plaster, and the roof was decked with slate stone shingles. So even if a house was shelled, it would not necessarily burn down. The content may burn, but not the house itself.

The people of Waxweiler were so grateful that the town survived the war, they built the sandstone monument of the Virgin Mary on top of a mountain which is still there to this day.

While my father was in the hospital in Heidelberg, the war front in that area came closer and closer. All the medical personnel evacuated and only one nurse remained behind to care for the wounded who could not be moved. She had hardly any supplies, but she did the best she could for the German and American wounded. When the American Army arrived, they wanted to take their own wounded and leave the Germans to their own devices. However, the wounded Americans were so grateful for the help of the nurse, they refused to leave her and the German wounded. The Army then provided food as well as medical personnel and supplies to the Germans. The German soldiers had been so starved, they couldn't eat all the food they were given. They began to hoard it for their families or for selling on the black marked. When the US Army found this out, they made them throw all the food in a ditch and burned it. My father, however, managed to keep a 50-pound sack of sugar hidden. This he took with him for his family when he left Heidelberg. He began his journey North by train to join his wife and children.

My mother knew that my father had been wounded, but she didn't know to what extent. She had received his letter from Heidelberg, but it was not in his own handwriting. The day before he was to arrive, a message was delivered to my mother by a soldier who had been travelling with my father. He let her know that my father and another soldier were arriving the next day at the Beverungen train station. He cautioned her to be prepared that my father had lost his right arm. My father had seen many women reject their husbands after serious injuries, and he had been hesitant to tell her. The train station was about 5 miles from Wehrden, where my mother was staying. The two soldiers walked the country road. My mother was unable to just wait at the house, so she began to walk towards Beverungen. In the distance she saw the two men. One of them had his right jacket sleeve pinned up and she knew it was her husband. She began to run towards him, and when he saw her, he ran, too. For my mother, having her husband back, meant the world. His amputation, she foresaw, would change their lives, but it wouldn't change her love.

A few weeks earlier in Wehrden, one morning my mother opened the front door of the house and found herself facing an American tank with its heavy cannon pointed at the front door. It scared her terribly. Americans came and billeted in the main part of the house, and the German civilians had to make room for them. She found out soon though, that the Americans were friendly towards civilians and especially to the children. They gave her canned peaches for Rudolf and Irmburg. It was such an unexpected special treat that 75 years later, our family still remembers this can of peaches.

My parents then began their trek back to Waxweiler. They loaded 8-month old Irmburg and 3-year old Rudolf and their few belongings onto a handcart. They walked, took the train when they could, hitched rides on trucks and walked some more. Great was the joy of my grandparents when they finally arrived in Waxweiler. They opened their home to them although it was already filled to the rafters.

My parents then started to build their home two doors down from my grandparents, with my maternal grandmother and aunts living in the middle house with the great-aunts from my father's side. Nobody had money, so everything was obtained by bartering. My father always said that our house was built with bacon and butter. My family sowed hats which they bartered with farmers for bacon and butter. My father then bartered that for construction materials and labor. He also sometimes smuggled food from the American to the French occupation sector to the city of Cologne where food was very scarce. He bartered there for cloth to sow more hats. My father helped to build that house with his own single remaining hand. My mother often dreaded it when he climbed a ladder, holding a bucket of mortar in his hand. They eventually finished enough of the house to move in and my sweet sister Hildegard was born at home in 1948.

When my father's right arm was amputated, the doctors had saved his wedding ring, but he never felt comfortable wearing it after losing it in Russia. Because he still was very thin, my mother wore both rings. One Saturday, after a full day of spring cleaning, she noticed that both rings were gone. Everyone retraced her steps and searched every nook and cranny of the house, even the ditch where she had poured out the mop water. She had stuffed fresh straw in mattresses that day, but after feeling through all the straw, the rings were nowhere to be found. Later that year, when the root vegetables in the garden had ripened, my mother pulled up a carrot and saw the glimmer of gold. She brushed the dirt off the carrot and there they were. The carrot had grown right through both rings. She remembered then, that she had used the old straw from the mattresses as mulch in the garden.

After my parents passed away, the rings went to my brother where they reside in his nightstand and remind him often of how strange life on this planet can be.

My father's dream of being a clothing designer had been utterly crushed. Now he could no longer draw designs or sow the intricate tuxedos and swallow-tail dress coats he had learned to make. He couldn't even sow work clothes or suits with his left hand. The only opportunity open to him was to be a meat inspector. His job was to go to every farm where animals had been slaughtered and inspect them for the health department. His transportation was a dilapidated bicycle with bad brakes. He had to navigate the surrounding mountains riding the bicycle with one hand.

My parents scraped by on his salary, but eventually in 1955 my mother opened a clothing store. It was the only store in Waxweiler that sold men's and ladies' apparel. However, unexpectedly, when Hildegard was already seven years old, my mother became pregnant with me. I was born in the hospital in Waxweiler on February 19, 1956. We lived in our house and she went to the storefront she rented in town, leaving me with a maid. In the afternoons and during vacations my siblings watched me.

I love my siblings. They have been nothing but good to me all my life. So, I don't remember the incident that happened when I was very small, but they have told me about it many times. They took me up to the statue of Mary at the top of the mountain, sat me down in the grass and played nearby. In my opinion my brother is the smartest person I know because he is so curious. Up on the mountain he wondered if fire could travel along a piece of dried grass from one little pile of hey to another. He laid it all out and set the first pile on fire. The hey must have been really dry because with one whoosh all the piles ignited, and so did the nearby grass. He had not noticed that he had built his experiment all the way around me. So now I was sitting in the middle of the fire. Rudolf jumped in to rescue me and my sisters quickly took off their jackets and beat out the fire.

In 1960 my mother moved her store to a different location where we could live in an upstairs apartment. This was much easier because I could be with my mother in the store during the day. We rented out the house they had built and later, in 1974 when my mother retired, we moved back in.

In 1975 my father received the biggest shock when he saw a car bearing USA license plates in front of our house. The car belonged to Bob Milewski, an American who was stationed in the nearby city of Bitburg.

I had moved in with Ina, a coworker from the travel agency in Bitburg. Ina and I loved to party, and Waxweiler was just too boring for me then. Bitburg had a movie theater and a disco. Unknowingly I had lived in the same house with Bob in Bitburg for a few months before we met.

Bob and Phillip, an Army buddy, rented a downstairs rear apartment from Ina's parents. They had a separate entrance, and all I knew of them was that they played loud rock music.

On Friday, July 25, 1975, I happened to sit on the front stoop of the house after work. The American's car pulled up and a soldier came walking towards the house. His head was down and he barely even glanced at me. He passed by to the rear entrance without saying a word. Then another soldier came out of the car. He started down the walkway and suddenly did a double take when he noticed me. He stopped for a minute and stared at me. Then he gave me a big smile, said "hi" and passed on.

That night we were having a birthday party for Ina's brother and I asked her to invite the Americans. The shy one didn't come, but I learned that the friendly one's name was Bob and he came. I had a bit of a hard time with his last name, and he couldn't pronounce my first name and promptly forgot it. We sat together and tried to communicate. I had only had one year of English in high school which I failed and had to repeat. My English had improved a little since working in Bitburg where 12,000 Americans were stationed in a town of 8,000 Germans. During the party we looked at a MADD magazine together and had some great laughs. I invited him to go to the disco with us but he declined. I was disappointed because I thought we had made a connection. He invited us to come down and listen to music the next night, but I had plans to be in Waxweiler for my mother's birthday. We told him we would come on Monday.

Monday came and Ina didn't want to go with me. So I went downstairs and Bob was alone as well. We sat, drank whiskey, smoked Kool cigarettes and listened to Pink Floyd. To my utter shock he asked me to marry him. He still didn't know my name and I thought he was kidding. I was only 19 and I told him "no" and that I wasn't planning on getting married until I was 26. I was intrigued by Bob and I saw him again the next day, and the next. And for three weeks straight he asked me every day if I would marry him.

He told me that when he had seen me for the first time he heard a voice say, "this is the woman you will marry." Well, I didn't hear that voice, and finally begged him to stop asking me and that I would let him know when he could ask again.

I really liked Bob. He was funny, strong-willed, and adventuresome. He was so different from me; he was outspoken and bold where I was compassionate and reserved. We had a great time hanging out together. I had always been insecure about my appearance, but Bob thought that was ridiculous. One day he made me stand in front of a mirror and say to myself "You are beautiful."

A few weeks into our relationship I brought Bob home to Waxweiler. I introduced him to my mother first, for my father wasn't home yet. My mother was gentle and friendly towards everyone. She invited Bob into the kitchen and I translated their conversation. Soon my father arrived and saw his car outside. My mother went to the door to tell him about their visitor. My father had never liked any of my boyfriends and this was no different. He gave Bob a rude greeting and went to the living room. He would not permit Bob to follow. I was quite upset. By now, Bob and I were living together and we drove back to Bitburg.

Bob was a "short-timer" in the Army. I learned a lot more English from him and some Army lingo as well. A short-timer is someone who is counting down the time when he gets out of the Military. Bob had a measuring tape and each day he cut off another inch to count down when he could go "back to the world" as he called the USA.

By the time September came around, he only had 100 days left in Germany, and I couldn't imagine life without Bob. On September 2nd, we went back to Waxweiler, met in the kitchen with my mother, and then went out to dinner at the Hotel am Schwimmbad owned by a distant cousin of mine. While waiting for our food Bob told me about his hometown, Buffalo, NY. He told me all about the severe winters there, the food, especially chicken wings, about the East Side, the Eastern Hills Mall, Tops, the Fruitbelt, Lake Erie and Bethlehem Steel. I wanted to know everything because I knew I would live there soon.

I finally said to Bob, "You can ask me again now." He was so thrilled. He asked me if I would marry him and this time I said "Yes."

During that same conversation we decided to stop drinking. Both of us had been drinking alcohol nearly every day, and we had discussed how alcohol had such a negative impact on both of our families. So, cold turkey, that night, we stopped, because we wanted to live our lives intentionally and raise a great family.

Our impending marriage changed Bob's short-timer plans. He made the ultimate sacrifice and extended his enlistment for four months.

Once my father knew that I would marry Bob he wanted to get to know him. Bob had many questions for him about the war. My father didn't speak English and Bob didn't speak German so any conversation they had was through my translation. I learned much about my father's war experience, things he had never talked about before. Bob kept asking question after question. My father took us to the Westwall and showed us the tank barriers and the remains of the bunker where he had been stationed.

My father and Bob were very much alike. Both were sarcastic and spoke their minds without filter. Except, I was the filter. I often translated their conversations somewhat diplomatically. My father didn't like the way Bob dressed and Bob didn't like how much my father drank. I refused to translate rudeness, and wouldn't you know it, they began to get along.

We got married in the church in Waxweiler on April 10, 1976. Bob left Germany on May 1, and I followed ten days later. I had never seen my father cry until he said "good bye" to Bob. I was amazed that he allowed me to marry Bob Milewski, an American GI, and that he learned to love him.

Once I moved to the States, it didn't take me long to learn that most Americans assumed Germans all had been avid Nazis during Hitler's reign. It offended me terribly when people jokingly gave me the Hail Hitler salute. I had grown up without any patriotism.

Once I was far away from Waxweiler I began to think about how beautiful it is. The older I've gotten the more I appreciate the close-knit community, the natural beauty, the convenience of walking everywhere, the food, the history, and the church.

On many visits back with my husband, kids and grandkids I have gained such respect for the people of the town and their determination to keep their culture alive. It was only when I was in a country that is barely 200 years old that I realized my little hometown of nearly 1,000 people has a history going back 2,000 years. The Roman ruins of the first settlement there, on top of one of the mountains would be a huge deal in America, but in Germany, surrounded by more impressive

Roman architecture, they are just there, not even fenced in, accessible to anyone.

As a teenager I had struggled with doubts whether Christianity was real. One day when I was 17, I walked into the church in Waxweiler and sat there all by myself in a pew. I looked around and I wondered if it all was real. Was there really a God? Was Jesus really the savior of the World? I asked God in my heart, "Are you really real? Or is this all just made up by people?" Suddenly the atmosphere around me changed. The sun shone through the restored stained glass windows and everything was so crisp and clear. I felt a joy deep inside. No one had ever told me that you could sense God's presence, so after a few minutes I got up, walked out and was convinced that I had just made that all up.

Two years later, when Bob and I lived together, we decided that there was no God. We just wanted to live without anyone telling us what to do. About a year after moving to Buffalo I began to work in a travel agency at the Thruway Mall. This was my first experience working in a big city with lots of sales people, customers and other shoppers. I began to adapt to the culture of materialism around me. I spent most of my paycheck on clothing and makeup and tried hard to fit in. I began to gossip, swear and join in with the backbiting that was going on. An emptiness inside made me miss my mother's goodness and the sense of community I had always taken for granted.

After a couple of years, I was offered a job at a different travel agency. The man who interviewed me, Gary Helffenstein, right away struck me as a really good guy. He hired me and then cut my interview short because he was going to church. I was flabbergasted. It was a Wednesday afternoon. He asked me if I went to church. I said, "No, I'm not that good of a Catholic."

From the day I started work at Wide World of Travel, Gary and his co-workers asked me every day if I would pray with them first thing in the morning. That made me very uncomfortable. I had never, ever prayed outside of a church. "No thank you," I would say. "You pray for me." And they did. They loved me. They showed mercy and grace to me. They included me in their families, and for six months they prayed for me. I stopped swearing and gossiping.

They were not Catholic, and up until this time, I had never learned anything about any other denomination. I did not want to be involved with something that wasn't real or true or was a cult. I asked Gary one day, "Do you believe in the Father, Son and Holy Spirit?" He said, "of course I do. I believe every word in the Bible."

Finally, on Friday, July 27, 1979, I was at work early and agreed to pray with them. We stood in a circle, holding hands. When Gary prayed and thanked God for me, I felt the same sense of God's presence I had at age 17 in the church in Waxweiler. It seemed that suddenly the box I had lived in all my life had opened up and there were more dimensions to life than I had realized. Later that day I accepted Jesus as my savior and asked him to come into my life. I had a powerful experience sensing both God's holiness and his mercy. I prayed from my heart for the first time. I remember the prayer: "Lord, whatever you have for me I want to receive, and whatever you desire from me, I want to give."

We started going to The Tabernacle in Orchard Park, NY, an Assemblies of God church. Six weeks later, Bob also surrendered to the love of God. We've been active followers of Jesus since then and now both work at Love Joy Church in Lancaster, NY.

We started attending Love Joy in 1988. The church was ten years old then. It amused me to think that my church in Waxweiler was started nearly 1,300 years ago. I began to think about how the Christian faith first came to Waxweiler around the year 700. Everyone in Waxweiler knows what happened because to this day they celebrate it every year at Pentecost Monday with a dance and a pilgrimage to Echternach in Luxemburg. A sandstone plaque at the church in Waxweiler records the legend as follows:

> Here admonished in vain St. Willibrord
> The pagans who danced on holy ground
> As penalty the dance became a bane
> Until they danced in penitence in Echternach

Having myself had experiences where I sensed the power of God, this legend became alive for me. When the internet became more prevalent and old documents became available, I researched the life of Willibrord. I saw how his life bridged history from the faith of St. Patrick of Ireland and St. Columbine of Iona in Scotland to the Synod of Whitby, the Anglo Saxon invasion of England all the way to the reign of Charlemagne. He influenced Charles the Hammer who stopped the invasion of the Muslims into Europe in 732AD and he was in Rome at a time of great conflict between the Roman Pope and the Byzantine Emperor, a time that heralded the great schism of the Church in 1054AD.

Willibrord was humble and he was powerful. The people in Waxweiler have experienced greatness of spirit and I pray they will continue to trust in the goodness of God.

I used to think Waxweiler was such a small place and nothing ever happened there, but I've found something better than a movie theater or a disco. I'm reminded of something C.S. Lewis said about the significance of smallness: *"Once in our world, a Stable had something in it that was bigger than our whole world."*

I'm finishing this appendix during the Coronavirus pandemic of 2020. As difficult as isolation and social distancing has been, at least there is no shellfire. In a time when the world is unsettled once again, I'm thankful to know that people of faith can not only rise above their circumstances but also be a support to others.

I thank Father Kiefer for his amazing journal. It's a record of conflict and pain, but also of faith under shellfire. I'm certain his influence led the way in shaping the mindsets of many. My family would not be the same if he had not stood strong against oppression. Thank you for that.

Uta (Irsch) Milewski

Translation of chorus of the 4th Century Latin hymn "Te Deus Laudeamus" one of the earliest known Christians hymns.

We praise thee, O God
We acknowledge thee to be the Lord.
All the earth doth worship thee
The Father everlasting.
To thee all Angels cry aloud
The Heavens, and all the Powers therein.
To thee Cherubim and Seraphim
Continually do cry,
Holy, Holy, Holy
Lord God of Sabaoth
Heaven and earth are full of the Majesty
Of thy glory.

Glossary

Ablution vessel = a small bowl of water on the altar for the priest to dip his fingers after handling consecrated wafers

Adolf Hitler = He rose to power as Chancellor of Germany in 1933 and later Führer in 1934. He committed suicide on April 30, 1945 and Nazi Germany unconditionally surrendered on May 7, 1945 thereby ending the Second Word War in Europe.

Advent = the four Sundays leading up to Christmas

All Saints Day = festival in honor of all the saints, held on November 1

All Souls Day = festival with prayers for the souls of the dead, held on November 2

Altar = in a Catholic Church, the table on which the Eucharist (communion) is celebrated by a priest

Altar cloth = a cloth that covers the altar

Blessed Sacrament = in the Catholic Church, the body and blood of Christ in the form of consecrated bread and wine

Dean = a Catholic priest holding a position of authority over other priests

Eifel = a low mountain range in western Germany and eastern Belgium

Gauamtsleiter = Regional Nazi leader

General absolution = in imminent danger of death a priest may grant all present and eligible Catholics absolution for sins without prior individual confession

Hitler Youth = the youth organization of the Nazi Party in Germany

Holy water font = a vessel containing holy water near the entrance of a church

Host = consecrated wafer of bread after transubstantiation

Jabo = short for "Jäger-Bomber," or "fighter-bomber" (literally, "hunter-bomber"), a fighter aircraft that has been modified for use as a light bomber or attack aircraft

Kreisleiter = the head Nazi of the county

Mother Superior = the head of a female religious community

National Socialism = short for National Socialist German Workers' Party

Nazi = short for Nationalsozialist, supporter of the National Socialist German Workers' Party

NSDAP = abbreviation for Nationalsozialistische Deutsche Arbeiterpartei which means National Socialist German Workers' Party

Ortsgruppenleiter = the head Nazi of a town or city

Panzer = tank

Prüm = this is both a river in the Eifel and a city near Waxweiler. The Prüm river runs through Waxweiler.

Sacristy = a room in a Catholic church where a priest prepares for a service, and where vestments and other things used in worship are kept

SS = short for Schutzstaffel which means Protective Squad. Began as a special guard for Adolf Hitler and other party leaders. The black-shirted SS members formed a smaller, elite group whose members also served as auxiliary policemen and, later, as concentration camp guards

Transubstantiation = in the Catholic Church, the change of substance by which the bread and wine offered in the sacrifice of the sacrament of the Eucharist during the Mass, become, in reality, the body and blood of Jesus Christ

Waffen-SS = the military branch of the Nazi Party's SS organization. Towards the end of the war many teenage men were drafted into the Waffen-SS without previously having been Nazi supporters

Waxweiler = a town of about 1,000 people with a history of nearly 2,000 years. Located in the Eifel region of Germany.

Wehrmacht = which means defense force, was the unified armed forces of Nazi Germany from 1935 to 1945. It consisted of the Heer (army), the Kriegsmarine (navy) and the Luftwaffe (air force)

Westwall = aka "Siegfried Line" was a German defensive tank barrier built during the 1930s opposite the French Maginot Line. The structure consisted of more than 18,000 bunkers, tunnels, anti-tank barriers and ditches and ran nearly 400 miles from the Dutch to the Swiss border.

Installation of Pastor Kiefer in Waxweiler, April 1936

*Visit by the bishop of the Roman Catholic diocese of Trier
The garlanded gateway leads to the rectory in Waxweiler*

Bishop's visit - Father Kiefer (right), Auxiliary bishop (middle)

The Nativity scene in the church in Waxweiler in 1950

The Nativity scene now. The hand-carved figures are 10 to 12 inches high and were obtained between 1924 and 1930. The backdrop was painted by a Waxweiler artist, Paula Francois, in 1924. The scene is set up annually in the church.

The Church in Waxweiler now

The Rectory was built in 1611. Photo from the late 1940's. The house in the background shows recent repairs.

Today the former rectory is used as Fellowship Hall for the Church

Adolf Hitler (in white coat) on August 27, 1938 at Waxweiler train station during a trip to inspect the Westwall

The sandstone statue of the Virgin Mary overlooking the town

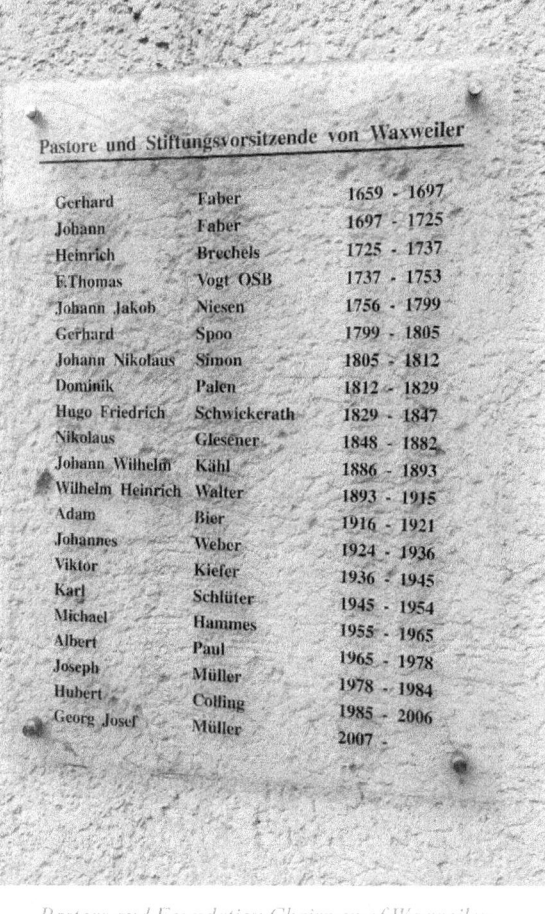

Pastors and Foundation Chairmen of Waxweiler

The Irsch family genealogy book sustained a Wehrmacht bullet hole while in a living room cupboard just prior to the American Army pulling into Waxweiler.

The Milewski men on a WW2 Sherman tank in Bastogne – 2012. Bob in the middle with his two sons who both served in the 82nd Airborne. Christopher (left) in Iraq and Stephan (right) in Afghanistan & Iraq

Tank barrier at the Westwall

The butter and bacon house on the left, aunt's in the middle and the Irsch grandparents' house on the right

The former Bekleidungshaus Irsch

Hirsch siblings Uta, Rudolf, Irmburg and Hildegard - 2018

Foreword of first edition

I am particularly pleased that I am allowed to make this journal of Pastor Kiefer available to the public.

Pastor Kiefer has left a valuable legacy of the last half of the war in a tactful, caring and helpful manner. This work sensitively depicts the worries and hardships of the people of our hometown during that time. For the people who did not have to experience this, it is an instructive example of peace education and symbolizes once again the community cohesion of the people of Waxweiler.

Special thanks go to all the people and departments who helped with this publication. I thank you all vicariously by thanking explicitly the sister of Pastor Kiefer, Miss Agnes Kiefer.

Klaus Juchmes

Leader of the Volksbildungswerk Waxweiler (1989)

Dear readers:

Today, we enjoy civilized freedom of which the generation before us, who suffered under Hitler's war, could not even have dreamed. As we all know, this freedom also affects church life. No one has any fear of being bullied or even "removed" from his job because he is going to church. It was different then, a commitment to God was a commitment against dictatorship.

We need to keep this in mind when we read the story of the end of the terrible war in our region. Each of us should do this and test our conscience as to whether we are truly grateful for the free German republic and democracy that we take for granted. This examination of conscience is necessary if we recall the meaning and duty of life. As a Christian, we owe this democracy a service: not great speeches, but personal courage and commitment when the Federal Republic is disrespected by ignorant people. This is the essential conclusion I draw from the journal of Pastor Kiefer.

Another lesson we should not overlook is gratitude. Kiefer's account calmly describes the hardships of the war. We know that after 1945, more than 130 wars all over the world cost innumerable lives, while for more than 40 years we have been allowed to live in peace, even though sometimes the noise of the fighter plans bothers us. Let's have compassion and pray for the people suffering from war today and gratitude for the peace that has been given to us by the policies of the West. Politics is by no means - as some people say dismissively - always a "dirty business." More often it is the performance by women and men at the local and the federal level, who are engaged in individual sacrifices, hardships, disappointments and ingratitude. We all know that, but do not put it into practice. It's easier and riskless to grumble.

The information provided by Kiefer's journal, which presents us with our hometown during a terrible phase of history, can give us insight that we're doing well, even if we have Unemployment or other troubles we temporarily can't solve.

Let's look back at the lives of those who, in their greatest material and physical distress, still loved our hometown, learned to love it even more intensely, and finally rebuilt it from rubble. That includes the refugees, who lost their homes and found a new home with us. Every Eifeler (Inhabitant of the Eifel region in which Waxweiler is located) may spend a quiet hour considering what it means for the heart and mind to be forever banished from his beloved home country and into an environment that seems alien, whose culture is unfamiliar, which never can replace the former home. Here, too, we have learned that today, two generations after the time Pastor Kiefer describes, no one distinguishes between locals and "strangers." The refugees who settled in our region have set an example of impeccable measure for peace worldwide, not by relying on revenge because of injustice, but because they peacefully began a new life, as God has granted us all.

Dear readers! Surely you do not resent a priest if he draws conclusions from Pastor Kiefer's journal for himself and those who may accept it.

Perhaps some of us thank God for the gift of our Eifel-region for the first time and for life in this beautiful countryside between Venn and Moselle. God bless us all and keep us in peace!

Your Hubert Colling

Priest and Dean of the parish of Waxweiler (1989)

www.ingramcontent.com/pod-product-compliance
Lightning Source LLC
Chambersburg PA
CBHW051954290426
44110CB00015B/2232